DATE DUE

JAN 17 2002			
JAN 17 2002			
FEB 01 2002			
FEB 21 2003			
MAR 06 2003			
JAN 22 04			
FEB 4 '04			
OCT 25 '04			
FEB 2 '05			
MAR 29 '05			
FEB 6 '07			
FEB 19 '07			
OCT 29 '12			

HIGHSMITH 45-220

THE THREE STOOGES

★ ★

POP CULTURE LEGENDS

THE THREE STOOGES

★ ★ ★ ★ ★ ★ ★ ★ ★ ★ ★ ★ ★ ★ ★ ★ ★ ★ ★

MARK AND ELLEN SCORDATO

CHELSEA HOUSE PUBLISHERS

New York ★ Philadelphia

CHELSEA HOUSE PUBLISHERS

EDITORIAL DIRECTOR Richard Rennert
EXECUTIVE MANAGING EDITOR Karyn Gullen Browne
COPY CHIEF Robin James
PICTURE EDITOR Adrian G. Allen
ART DIRECTOR Robert Mitchell
MANUFACTURING DIRECTOR Gerald Levine
ASSISTANT ART DIRECTOR Joan Ferrigno

Pop Culture Legends
SENIOR EDITOR Kathy Kuhtz Campbell
SERIES DESIGN Basia Niemczyc

Staff for **THE THREE STOOGES**
EDITORIAL ASSISTANT Scott D. Briggs
SENIOR DESIGNER Basia Niemczyc
PICTURE RESEARCHER Matthew Dudley
COVER ILLUSTRATION Hal Just

3 5 7 9 8 6 4

Library of Congress Cataloging-in-Publication Data

Scordato, Mark.
The Three Stooges/Mark and Ellen Scordato.
p. cm.—(Pop culture legends)
Includes bibliographical references and index.
ISBN 0-7910-2344-3
    0-7910-2369-9 (pbk.)
1. Three Stooges (Comedy team)—Juvenile literature. 2. Three
Stooges films—Juvenile literature. 3. Motion picture actors
and actresses—United States—Biography—Juvenile literature.
4. Comedians—United States—Biography—Juvenile literature.
[1. Three Stooges (Comedy team) 2. Actors and actresses.
3. Comedians.] I. Scordato, Ellen. II. Title. III. Series.
PN1995.9.T5S38. 1995   94-19343
791.43'028'0922—dc20   CIP
[B]   AC

FRONTISPIECE

In one of the Three Stooges
film shorts, Moe (left) and
Larry (right) prepare themselves
for an explosion as Curly
(center) is about to set the
blasting powder ablaze.

Contents ★ ★ ★ ★ ★ ★ ★ ★ ★ ★ ★ ★ ★ ★ ★ ★ ★ ★ ★

A Reflection of Ourselves

Leeza Gibbons

I ENJOY A RARE PERSPECTIVE on the entertainment industry. From my window on popular culture, I can see all that sizzles and excites. I have interviewed legends who have left us, such as Bette Davis and Sammy Davis, Jr., and have brushed shoulders with the names who have caused a commotion with their sheer outrageousness, like Boy George and Madonna. Whether it's by nature or by design, pop icons generate interest, and I think they are a mirror of who we are at any given time.

Who are *your* heroes and heroines, the people you most admire? Outside of your own family and friends, to whom do you look for inspiration and guidance, as examples of the type of person you would like to be as an adult? How do we decide who will be the most popular and influential members of our society?

You may be surprised by your answers. According to recent polls, you will probably respond much differently than your parents or grandparents did to the same questions at the same age. Increasingly, world leaders such as Winston Churchill, John F. Kennedy, Franklin D. Roosevelt, and evangelist Billy Graham have been replaced by entertainers, athletes, and popular artists as the individuals whom young people most respect and admire. In surveys taken during each of the past 15 years, for example, General Norman Schwarzkopf was the only world leader chosen as the number-one hero among high school students. Other names on the elite list joined by General Schwarzkopf included Paula Abdul, Michael Jackson, Michael Jordan, Eddie Murphy, Burt Reynolds, and Sylvester Stallone.

★ ★

More than 30 years have passed since Canadian sociologist Marshall McLuhan first taught us the huge impact that the electronic media have had on how we think, learn, and understand—as well as how we choose our heroes. In the 1960s, Pop artist Andy Warhol predicted that there would soon come a time when every American would be famous for 15 minutes. But if it is easier today to achieve Warhol's 15 minutes of fame, it is also much harder to hold on to it. Reputations are often ruined as quickly as they are made.

And yet, there remain those artists and performers who continue to inspire and instruct us in spite of changes in world events, media technology, or popular tastes. Even in a society as fickle and fast moving as our own, there are still those performers whose work and reputation endure, pop culture legends who inspire an almost religious devotion from their fans.

Why do the works and personalities of some artists continue to fascinate us while others are so quickly forgotten? What, if any, qualities do they share that enable them to have such power over our lives? There are no easy answers to these questions. The artists and entertainers profiled in this series often have little more in common than the enormous influence that each of them has had on our lives.

Some offer us an escape. Artists such as actress Marilyn Monroe, comedian Groucho Marx, and writer Stephen King have used glamour, humor, or fantasy to help us escape from our everyday lives. Others present us with images that are all too recognizable. The uncompromising realism of actor and director Charlie Chaplin and folk singer Bob Dylan challenges us to confront and change the things in our world that most disturb us.

Some offer us friendly, reassuring experiences. The work of animator Walt Disney and late-night talk show host Johnny Carson, for example, provides us with a sense of security and continuity in a changing world. Others shake us up. The best work of composer John Lennon and actor James Dean will always inspire their fans to question and reevaluate the world in which they live.

It is also hard to predict the kind of life that a pop culture legend will lead, or how he or she will react to fame. Popular singers Michael Jackson

★ ★

and Prince carefully guard their personal lives from public view. Other performers, such as popular singer Madonna, enjoy putting their private lives before the public eye.

What these artists and entertainers do share, however, is the rare ability to capture and hold the public's imagination in a world dominated by mass media and disposable celebrity. In spite of their differences, each of them has somehow managed to achieve legendary status in a popular culture that values novelty and change.

The books in this series examine the lives and careers of these and other pop culture legends, and the society that places such great value on their work. Each book considers the extraordinary talent, the stubborn commitment, and the great personal sacrifice required to create work of enduring quality and influence in today's world.

As you read these books, ask yourself the following questions: How are the careers of these individuals shaped by their society? What role do they play in shaping the world? And what is it that so captivates us about their lives, their work, or the images they present?

Hopefully, by studying the lives and achievements of these pop culture legends, we will learn more about ourselves.

A Stooge by Any Other Name

I

THE BEGINNING of the Three Stooges as a comedy team is as wild and bizarre as any one of the more than 200 films that they made—films that have touched, or at least poked, the lives of millions. Initially, the Stooges were exactly what their name implies: stooges, the butt of jokes for a well-known comedian named Ted Healy. Early in the 1930s, they decided to break with Healy—a momentous decision on their part, considering that they had worked with him for years onstage and in short movies at the Metro-Goldwyn-Mayer (MGM) studio in Hollywood. The Stooges—Moe Howard, Larry Fine, and Curly Howard—made the break because they felt ready to go out on their own. But they were anxious. They had always been the second banana and had never starred in their own major show or movie. Ted Healy had connections, fame, and respect; but he also had many personal problems, and the Stooges did all they could with him until it was time to break away.

It was 1934, and the United States was still deep within the Great Depression. People were hungry and jobs were scarce, but Hollywood was

Moe Howard, Larry Fine, and Curly Howard slyly look around a column in a scene from one of their two-reel films. In more than 200 film shorts and over 40 years of comedy, the Three Stooges made their surreal slapstick forever appealing to fans.

In *Plane Nuts,* comedian Ted Healy (standing) tries to eavesdrop on the Stooges as they whisper in a huddle. Healy had top billing in all of his ventures with the Stooges, commanding a high salary out of which he paid the trio a small portion.

thriving. No matter how desperate people were, they never hesitated to throw down a nickel to watch their favorite movie heroes every Saturday afternoon. Poverty was on every corner, but up on the movie screen there was a funny, exciting, romantic world, filled with beautiful people and outrageous comedians, going on thrilling adventures all over the globe. There were so many weighty problems in the real world. Moe, Larry, and Curly wanted to make people laugh and, perhaps, help them forget their worries for a while.

After signing the papers separating them from Ted Healy, the Stooges left the MGM studio lot. Moe departed from one gate, Larry from another. They were to meet with Curly later that day at Moe's apartment to discuss just what they were going to do. The future held a lot of promise for them, but they knew it would not be easy to achieve their dream. Before he reached his car, Moe was stopped by a Hollywood agent named Walter Kane. Kane knew about the split from Healy, and he told Moe that he wanted to take him right then and there to Columbia Pictures and try to obtain a movie contract for the Stooges. Moe could not believe it; it had been only a few minutes since they had severed their ties from Healy, and now Moe was about to meet one of the most prominent men in Hollywood: Harry Cohn, the head of Columbia Pictures.

Cohn had a reputation as a vicious negotiator and a ruthless man; among the nicknames hung on him were Harry the Horror, White Fang, and King Cohn. He had tried to make it himself on the vaudeville circuit back in the early 1910s, but he had failed. Instead he rose from a job as a personal secretary at Universal Studios to creator (along with his brother Jack) of his own major motion picture studio, Columbia Pictures. He offered Moe a one-picture contract for the Stooges on the spot. It was for a short film, known as a two-reeler, for which the Three Stooges would be paid $1,500. If Columbia liked the picture, it would have 60 days to sign the Stooges to a long-term deal. Moe was ecstatic. This was their chance. He was hardly able to wait to

Healy and His Stooges appear in a scene from *Plane Nuts*. In 1934, Curly Howard, Moe Howard, and Larry Fine decided that the time was right to break away from Healy and try to make it on their own.

Larry, Curly, and Moe sneak up on Harry Cohn, the head of Columbia Pictures. The Three Stooges signed with Columbia when they left Healy and would eventually make about 190 films with the studio.

convey the news to Larry and Curly. But as it turned out, Moe was not the only one with news to tell.

After Larry left MGM, he was approached by a Hollywood agent named Joe Rivkin, who took him to Universal Studios in order to get the Stooges a contract. There he and Larry met with studio head Carl Laemmle Jr.; Harry Cohn had been a personal secretary to Laemmle's

father 16 years earlier. The son of a German immigrant who had started out as a drugstore errand boy before opening his own nickelodeon, eventually building it into a movie empire, Carl junior had been put in charge of production at Universal in 1929, when he was only 21. He offered Larry a contract for the Stooges, and Larry accepted it. Thus, within minutes of putting their destiny in their own hands, the Stooges had signed mutually exclusive contracts with two of the most important people in all of Hollywood.

As soon as the Three Stooges were together at Moe's apartment, Moe told them the story of his meeting with Harry Cohn. But he did not get the reaction he had counted on, for Larry then blurted out his story about his meeting with Carl Laemmle Jr. The three of them were dumbfounded. The next day, a series of meetings and phone calls determined that Moe had signed his contract with Columbia about three hours earlier than Larry had signed his with Universal. The Stooges belonged to Columbia.

Having been with Ted Healy for so long, Larry and Curly questioned whether the Stooges could make it on their own. But Moe, as the new unofficial leader of the group, convinced them that it would all be for the best, and their first decision was to change their name. No longer would they be Ted Healy and His Stooges; from then on they would be known as the Three Stooges. They remained the Three Stooges for nearly four decades, and the mere mention of their name can instantly conjure up their unmistakable images of eye-poking, pie-throwing, seltzer-squirting zaniness.

2 A Stooge Grows in Brooklyn

THE STORY OF THE THREE STOOGES begins with the account of the lives of the Horwitz brothers of Brooklyn, New York, at the dawn of the 20th century. The roots of the brothers' family were in Eastern Europe, and their parents arrived in the United States with the great flood of immigrants during the late 19th century.

Solomon Gorovitz was born on November 4, 1872, in Kovno, Lithuania, which was at that time part of the Russian Empire. Jennie Gorovitz, his distant cousin, was born on April 4, 1869, in Vilna, Lithuania. Solomon left Kovno to attend school in Vilna. He studied at the rabbinical seminary there and lived with his cousins. Just before Solomon was to graduate from rabbinical school, gangs of Russian soldiers roamed through Lithuania to force young men to join the Russian army, which turned out to be years of hard service for many. The family realized that Solomon was in danger of being conscripted. The Gorovitzes were Jews, and they knew that Jews who were forced to join the army endured not only terrible conditions but also

Dressed in childlike footed pajamas, the Three Stooges stick out their tongues in a scene from one of their two-reelers. Moses "Moe" Horwitz was six years older than his youngest brother, Jerome ("Curly"), and recollected in his memoirs that he and his brothers caused endless trouble in school when they were children.

17

forced conversions to Christianity. Solomon had to flee Lithuania. Nearly every would-be emigrant had heard stories of the riches and religious tolerance that could be found in the United States, so the family decided to send Solomon to America. Thinking they would make a good match, the family quickly arranged a marriage between Solomon and his cousin Jennie (a common practice at the time), the couple wed, and then they hastily set out for America.

The journey, first through Europe on foot and then across the Atlantic Ocean on a crowded steamer, was harsh, but the newlyweds landed safely in New York City in 1890. Like many other refugees, the Gorovitzes' surname was misunderstood by immigration authorities, and they wound up with the name Horwitz instead. It did not seem to make much difference to them, for they had more important matters to attend to. Solomon and Jennie settled in with Jennie's brother Julius, who lived in Brooklyn (after immigrating to the United States earlier), and they started a family. Their first son, Irving, was born in 1891; their second son, Benjamin, followed in 1893. Samuel "Shemp" Horwitz was born on March 17, 1895; Moses "Moe" Horwitz on June 19, 1897; and Jerome "Curly" Lester Horwitz, the baby, was born on October 22, 1903. (Shemp, Moe, and Curly took the last name Howard as their stage name in the 1910s.)

Solomon tried hard to make money to support his burgeoning family, but he had no aptitude for business. The energetic Jennie invested the little money he earned. She bought and sold real estate, all the while sewing, cooking, cleaning, and taking care of her brood of rambunctious boys. She became so successful that she was able to move the young family into their own house in Bath Beach, Brooklyn, a seaside resort area where many members of the theatrical profession spent their vacations.

In the 1970s, Moe wrote of his childhood memories in his autobiography, *Moe Howard and the 3 Stooges*. He recalled how he and his brothers caused endless trouble in school and chaos almost everywhere else. He remembered Shemp as "an impossible crybaby, a stocking and pants destroyer, a general creator of disturbances."

Shemp, who got his name because of the way his mother called him with her accent, was not the only troublemaker. Moe had problems of his own. According to family lore, Jennie had wanted her fourth child to be a girl. Moe was not, obviously, but he did have long, curly hair, which Jennie delighted in brushing and arranging in long sausage-shaped curls. The style was acceptable for toddlers in those days, but Jennie kept Moe's hair long

As a child, Moe had to defend himself daily from his classmates' teasing about his long, curly black hair. Unable to bear the brunt of the jeers any longer, Moe took scissors and clipped the curls off—the resulting cut became his trademark.

19

During Moe, Shemp, and Curly's youth, Coney Island, a resort area of Brooklyn, New York, located along the Atlantic Ocean, was popular for its boardwalk, hotels, and amusement parks. The Horwitz brothers passed a lot of time on the beaches of Brooklyn entertaining their friends.

well beyond the toddler stage. Even his brothers taunted him about it.

By the time Moe went to kindergarten at the age of six, he was forced to fight daily to defend himself from the jeers of his classmates. For five long years Moe endured incessant teasing about his hair. Supposedly, despondent after a particularly brutal episode, he went over to a friend's house where he made a fateful decision. Moe picked up a pair of scissors, shut his eyes, and cut off the curls, working carefully around his head. After he finished and looked in the mirror, his friends screamed with laughter. His hair looked like a black bowl turned upside down on his head. Moe's trademark haircut was born.

By the time Moe reached his teens, he was deeply interested in show business, to his mother's dismay. Solomon was devoutly religious and very active at the local synagogue, which was all right with Jennie, but she wanted her boys to be successful businessmen or professional men such as doctors and lawyers. Instead of applying themselves in school, Moe and Shemp were the beach bums of their day. They spent hours on the shore in Brooklyn, entertaining their friends with humorous pranks, singing and playing the ukulele (a small Hawaiian-style guitar), and finagling dates with girls. Shemp seems to have been the funnyman, Moe the straight man. Often their brother Jerome, known as Babe, tagged along. Babe was an attractive little boy, and

as the youngest, was rather spoiled by Jennie and his older
brother Moe. Babe was an adamant dog lover, even as an
adult, and often picked up strays to care for them. He was
always beautifully dressed in the latest styles. He idolized
his older brothers and admired their ability to attract
attention with their impromptu performances and gags.
But being very shy around strangers, he rarely took part
in the fun and only watched.

Moe and Shemp yearned to one day perform in front
of a real, paying audience. However, show business at the
beginning of the 20th century was tremendously different
from what it is today. Before television and radio, popular
entertainment was almost all live. In the 1910s, there was
no such thing as Hollywood, a broadcasting network, or
cable television. Instead people flocked to theaters,
vaudeville houses, and an exciting new entertainment
called the moving pictures.

Theatergoers had a wide range of entertainment to
choose from. They could see serious dramas, witty
sketches, lavish musicals, and Shakespearean plays. Popular plays also included melodramas (sentimental tales of
good and evil), silly comedies full of outlandish plot
twists, and racy musicals featuring scantily clad female
dancers. These entertainments filled people's need for
diversion, just as contemporary television movies and
situation comedies do today. However, there was one
type of stage entertainment that was popular in the late
19th and early 20th centuries that has no true parallel
today: vaudeville.

Vaudeville was a very special kind of theater. A vaudeville performance could be composed of short comedic
skits, dramatic recitations, musical performances, blackface skits (featuring white performers in black makeup
ridiculing blacks), funny songs, contortionist acts, magic
demonstrations, trained animal acts, jugglers, and more.
It was hugely popular and dominated the business.

Movies then were only black and white, all silent, and
very short. Most were made in New York. They were new
and interesting, but at the time no one knew if they would
last and grow the way vaudeville had.

Moe seemed very nearly obsessed with show business.
He often skipped school so he could spend his time in
the theaters. At the age of 12, he discovered that one of
the many small movie companies in New York, Vitagraph, had its studios only a half-hour subway ride from
the Horwitz home. Moe hung out at Vitagraph, ran
errands for the actors for free, and was eventually cast in
short films, even appearing with baseball great Honus
Wagner. He loved it.

A film still from *Amateur
Night in London* (1930)
depicts the Rego Twins,
a popular vaudeville act.
Vaudeville dominated show
business when Moe was
a teenager, and he became
consumed by the idea
of performing onstage in
a comedy act.

In the late 1940s, Moe, his brother Shemp, and Larry act in a stunt involving seltzer bottles. Shemp enjoyed entertaining as much as Moe did; however, as a teenager he was less convinced than his brother that he could make a living at vaudeville and decided to attend a trade school instead.

In the summer of 1909, while singing with friends on the beach, Moe met a young man named Lee Nash. They became fast friends, although their backgrounds were very different. Lee came from a wealthy Scotch-Irish family who lived on the fashionable Upper West Side of Manhattan and summered at the Brooklyn shore. Moe recalled that he and Lee, along with some other friends, engaged in a number of stunts, some more harebrained than others. In the summer of 1912, they joined a diving show called Annette Kellerman's Diving Girls. They stuffed newspapers in the top of their long, one-piece bathing suits and performed alongside Kellerman's girls,

24

somewhat uncomfortably because the sodden news-papers slipped down to their waist after each dive and required swift, discreet adjustment. They quit the show after one of the girls broke her neck in a mistimed dive.

Shemp liked the idea of being in front of an audience as much as Moe did but seemed less sure of show business as a career. He did not finish high school and instead attended a trade school, then worked at a number of odd jobs, including as a plumber, newsboy, and bowling-pin setter. He and Moe sometimes performed at amateur nights and local dance halls, and eventually Shemp seri-ously began to consider earning a living from his ability to make people laugh. In 1914, he began to work on the rudiments of a blackface act to be performed with Moe. As ever, their youngest brother, Babe, was their biggest fan.

Nothing could keep Moe away from the theater. Every week he pored over *Billboard*, then *the* show business newspaper, as he recalled in his memoirs. In 1914, he thought he saw his chance and answered an advertise-ment for a "young man—average height to play juvenile parts" needed by a company of actors who performed during the summers on a showboat, the *Sunflower*, on the Mississippi River. The ad requested a photograph be mailed as an application. Moe was only five feet four inches tall. Undeterred, he removed a picture of a hand-some, taller neighbor from the wall and sent it off. In reply came train tickets and the promise of a job. Shemp was appalled, certain his brother would wind up in jail. Moe went anyway, and, of course, the company manager was aghast when he compared Moe to the picture he had received. Yet he seems to have been a kindly man, and he let Moe do odd jobs for the actors. When he offered Moe a few bit parts, Moe excelled in them. The showboat company performed the old plays he had seen over and over again in Brooklyn, and he knew the parts inside out.

He spent two summers there, gaining valuable experience and earning a good salary.

Probably during the winter of 1915–16 (there is some doubt about the exact time), Moe and Shemp signed on with a theatrical agent and finally appeared on the vaudeville stage. They were to perform a blackface number under the name Howard and Howard at the Mystic Theater on Fifty-third Street and Third Avenue in

The marquee at Brooklyn's Bushwick Theatre includes the names of Howard and Howard, circa 1914. Shemp and Moe Howard worked up a blackface act and signed with a theatrical agent, who booked their routine in the New York City area.

26

Manhattan. Appearing last and after four acts, they had about 12 minutes to do their routine. But theirs was not an auspicious beginning.

As they stepped in front of the footlights for the first time, they began their routine. The first jokes were met with dead silence. So were the rest of their jokes. Moe and Shemp bowed out as the audience headed for the exits. They realized, sadly, that the manager had hired them to clear out the theater so that more paying customers could come in and fill the seats. The performances were continuous, and the manager's profit depended on turning over the bodies in the seats as efficiently as possible. They bore the indignity of this treatment for the entire length of their contract, mercifully only three days.

Still, Moe and Shemp persevered. The act broke up briefly when Shemp was drafted for military service in World War I but re-formed soon after, when Shemp was discharged as a bed wetter. Their act met more success as they gained experience, and at last they felt they had truly made it in vaudeville. The brothers played for the well-known Loew's and Radio-Keith-Orpheum (RKO) theaters, which were rival organizations. In the RKO theaters, they performed in blackface; in the Loew's theaters, without makeup. The world of vaudeville was bizarre at times, and Shemp and Moe met all sorts of people—German acrobats, affable contortionists, temperamental singers, and shady managers who were reluctant to pay them.

Shemp and Moe continued as Howard and Howard until 1922, when Moe's childhood friend Lee Nash, who had taken the stage name Ted Healy, appeared at the Prospect Theater in Brooklyn. The Howard brothers were about to enter a whole new world of celebrity.

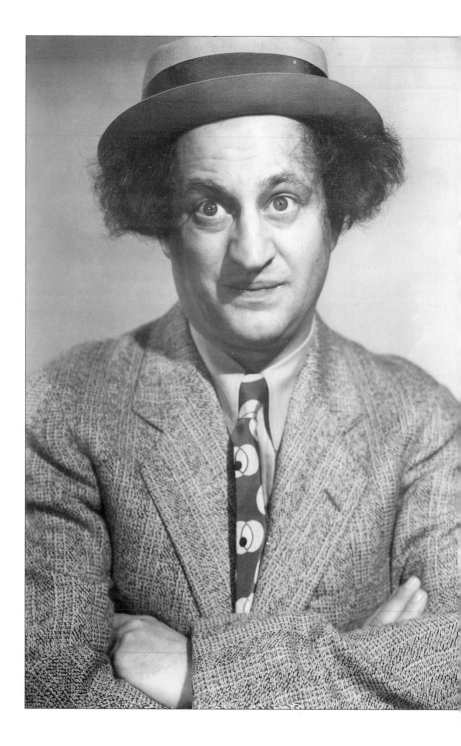

3 Loco Boys Make Good

BUMPING INTO TED HEALY at the Prospect Theater turned out to be a great stroke of luck for the stage-crazed Moe. The participants' recollections vary. Some recall that Moe and Shemp went to the theater to see Healy's act; others remember that they were there to perform their own act. One story holds that Healy's acrobats had walked out, leaving time to fill, and Healy called Shemp and Moe up from the audience. Their ad-libs were impressively hilarious. Moe and Shemp joined Healy's act in 1922 and were a big hit. Healy was already a popular vaudevillian. Known for his fine voice and trademark battered hat, his comedy was broad—today it might be considered brutal. Moe would "accidentally" pull down Healy's pants, and the crowd would roar its approval. Or Shemp would offer a bite of his pear to Healy, who would decline the offer and eventually smash the pear into Shemp's twisting face. Healy discovered that he worked much better off of stooges and explained years later that "a stooge always comes in handy when you feel like throwing something at somebody. Whenever I'm in doubt or feel mixed up, I always hit the nearest stooge. Makes me feel better. Nothing like it.

Louis Feinberg, or Larry Fine, grew up in Philadelphia, Pennsylvania. Like the Horwitz brothers, Larry loved comedy as a teenager and entered amateur night competitions.

Hollywood's tired of yes-men. That's why the stooge is coming into his own. A stooge is a guess-man. You can never know what he's going to do next." Healy was soon making $3,500 a week—a huge sum of money in those days. Out of this amount he gave Moe and Shemp $100 apiece. The problem of low pay would plague the Stooges until they were finally on their own.

Jennie Horwitz was against the boys' show business careers from the start. Solomon barely spoke around the house, as family members recalled, so what Jennie said carried immense weight. She was afraid her sons would never be able to support themselves in the theater, which she considered a low-class profession. Ted Healy himself implored her to let the boys be part of his act, and Jennie relented only after he agreed to make a charitable donation to their synagogue.

For the next three years the act plugged away under a variety of names, most of which began "Ted Healy and. . . ." Healy loved to drink, and, despite Prohibition, which made the manufacture and sale of alcohol illegal from 1920 to 1933, he managed to spend many a night out—all night, traveling from speakeasy to speakeasy (as the places that sold illegal alcohol were called). During this time, Shemp appeared alone with Healy in a few popular J. J. Shubert musicals.

In 1925, both Moe and Shemp decided to marry their girlfriends. First, Moe married Helen Schonberger, whom he had met in Brooklyn. A few months later, Shemp married Gertrude "Babe" Frank. Marriage, of course, meant new responsibilities, for each looked forward to starting a family.

That same year they met another man who would have a great effect on their future. During a night out in Chicago, Ted, Moe, and Shemp went to Rainbo Gardens, a nightclub and jai-alai fronton (arena). The nightclub featured an act in which a strange-looking man in a tuxedo and long tails played the violin, told jokes, and performed a Russian dance. Impressed by the fellow's wild humor, Ted and the two Howards met with the performer, Larry Fine, and asked him to join their group. Larry was offered $100 a week—$90 for the act itself and $10 to get rid of the fiddle. Larry, however, had only recently signed a seven-year contract with the nightclub. The next night the police closed the club because it was serving alcohol. Larry no longer had a binding contract and was free to join the new group.

Louis Feinberg (his stage name was Larry Fine) was born on October 5, 1902, in South Philadelphia, Pennsylvania. Like Solomon and Jennie Gorowitz, Joseph Frienchicov, Larry's father, had emigrated from Russia because of anti-Semitism. He was a successful watchmaker and jeweler who took Feinberg as his surname upon his arrival in the United States, when he found out that his brother Nathan had been using that name. In Philadelphia, Joseph met Fannie Lieberman, and the couple got married. Larry was their first child, followed by Moe, Phillip, and Lyla. According to family members, Larry was a born comic who seemed to want to please an audience since the days when he wore diapers. When he was only two years old, he danced for admiring relatives in his parents' jewelry shop. After entertaining them for a few moments, young Larry fell through a glass case. Fortunately, he was not hurt, but that might have been the first pratfall of his hilarious career.

He was forced to learn the violin at the age of four as therapy after he burned his arm badly with acid in the jewelry shop. What started as rehabilitation eventually became a lifelong love. Music seemed to run in the family; when Joseph had been drafted by the army in Russia, he escaped persecution by joining the army band as a horn player. Larry grew to be a proficient musician, able to play many different instruments (including a homemade violin, constructed from a cigar box, a broom handle, and strings, that he played like a cello). He played first violin in his grammar school orchestra, and when he was 10 he soloed at a children's concert in Philadelphia, performing *Humoresque* by Dvořák. As he got older, he entered amateur night competitions, which he usually won.

His younger brother Moe, who spent much time with Larry backstage at amateur nights, recalls him as an excellent comedian as well as a somewhat successful boxer and singer. Larry's parents supported his interest in music, but his father preferred that his son play classical compositions. Larry had other plans. His first big vaudeville performance panned out well in 1921 (or 1917, according to Moe Feinberg) in Gus Edwards' Newsboy Sextette. He met several other entertainers there, and together they formed an act called the Haney Sisters (who were singers, dancers, and comedians) and Fine. Larry liked the Haney sisters—especially Mabel, whom he later married. But Larry's life changed the night he met Moe, Shemp, and Healy. The Horwitz brothers and Feinberg had grown up around vaudeville, loved music, and came from similar backgrounds—hardworking, exuberant immigrant families. Shemp, Moe, and especially Larry admired actor-comedian Charlie Chaplin and singer Al Jolson. With the Howards, Larry shared a very particular, very physical, and wholly bizarre sense of humor.

Throughout the next few years, the group's name changed. (Among the names they called themselves were Ted Healy and His Three Southern Gentlemen and Ted Healy and His Gang.) One member or another would drop out for a time, but there was always one constant: when together onstage, they were extremely funny. Their act continued to get more and more outrageous, and people flocked to see them. Healy and the Stooges wrestled with bears, led a parade of cats across the stage, took

Actor and director Charlie Chaplin is seen here in the 1915 silent movie *The Tramp.* Shemp, Moe, and Larry revered Chaplin, whose agility and sense of timing in comedy had no equal.

away ladders to leave someone hanging from the top of the stage curtains. The sillier the idea, the more they liked it, and the more the audience laughed and cheered. The group toured across the country, but they were especially popular in New York and California.

In 1927, when Healy and Shemp left to do the Broadway musical revue *A Night in Spain,* Moe decided to spend more time with his wife and new daughter, Joan. Larry also took a break by marrying Mabel Haney. During this time away from the stage, Moe tried his hand at real estate. He invested more than $20,000 in land and built houses in Brooklyn. The houses he constructed turned out to be too expensive for that neighborhood, and he lost almost all of his investment. After a second business failed, Moe realized that he had to return to show business, where he felt he belonged. He called Ted Healy, who immediately gave Moe the opportunity to rejoin the group. Healy and his stooges had been invited to perform in a new musical with the Shubert organization.

Choreographer and director Busby Berkeley worked with Healy and the Stooges in the 1929 Broadway revue *A Night in Venice*. Critics raved about their comedy act in the revue and considered it the best part of the production.

In 1929, Ted Healy and His Stooges appeared in *A Night in Venice*, a Broadway revue directed and choreographed by Busby Berkeley, who went on to direct some of the most lavish and successful Hollywood musicals of the 1930s, including *Forty-second Street, The Gold Diggers of 1933,* and *For Me and My Gal.* Critic Brooks Atkinson, in the *New York Times,* enthusiastically called the Stooges "three of the frowziest numbskulls ever assembled. . . . a masterpiece of slapstick comedy. . . . the best number."

That October, the stock market crashed, marking the start of the Great Depression. The show closed—but not before the Stooges had made an impact on the entertainment world. Even their name itself took on a life of its own. In her New York Theater column, writer Alison Smith wrote that the word *stooges* "is a vaguely descriptive little word, yet we haven't yet been able to determine just what it describes. . . . Wherever it came from, it is now definitely fixed in theatrical vocabulary and you don't have to read Variety to recognize these grease-paint Sancho Panzas, dumbly loyal to the master mind of their leader." The group was rewarded for its success in *A Night in Venice* when a scout from Fox Studios, who had seen the show, signed Healy and the Stooges to appear in the film *Soup to Nuts* (1930).

Ted Healy accepted a smaller salary than usual, only $1,250 per week, in order to make the picture. Each Stooge received $150 per week from Healy. The Stooges (whom Ephraim Katz in *The Film Encyclopedia* says were billed as The Racketeers) played both wacky firemen and Mexican revolutionaries in the film, whose script was cowritten by the renowned cartoonist Rube Goldberg. The Stooges' work in the film persuaded Fox to offer the three sidekicks their own seven-year contract. When Healy found out about the deal he was furious, and he implored Fox not to break up his act. He knew how much he needed his stooges. Fox decided to rescind its offer to the Stooges.

An outraged Moe convinced Shemp and Larry that they could make it as a trio without Healy, and they soon were doing shows billed as the Three Lost Souls. Healy, meanwhile, tried to make it with three new stooges, but his show was a disaster. His nights of drinking turned Healy into an alcoholic, and his career suffered. He needed his old group back. Yet what he did next merely alienated Healy further from the Stooges.

As Moe, Larry, and Shemp prepared to play at the Hippodrome in New York City, Healy sued them to prevent the Stooges from using any of the old material they had developed with him. The suit also claimed that they could not use Healy's name in their ads, which billed them as "former associates of Ted Healy." However, theater owner J. J. Shubert claimed that the material was developed as part of the Shubert enterprise, and he signed over the rights to Moe, Larry, and Shemp, so Healy's suit failed. Healy then hired some goons to threaten to beat up the Stooges if they continued to use "Healy's" material.

However, the Stooges were already using more and more of their own original skits, writing new bits at a feverish pace. Their efforts were not born simply from the fear of lawsuits or bodily harm. They yearned to establish their own identity, and without Healy they now had the freedom to try out whatever they wanted. Unfortunately, vaudeville routines were not scripted, and none of the Stooges' were ever filmed, so the development of their material can be evaluated only by reading the reviews. Luckily, as part of Healy's lawsuit, an observer was sent to watch the Stooges' act and write it down. The routine described is one in which the Stooges are called onstage by a master of ceremonies, or emcee. Part of the skit ran as follows:

[Moe]: Hello, Shemp. Where are you going?
[Shemp]: I'm going fishing.
[Moe]: Have you got worms?
[Shemp]: Yeah, I got 'em, but I'm going anyway.

([Moe] pulls [Shemp]'s nose. [Shemp] slaps [Moe]; [Moe] pokes [Larry]'s eyes. General hubbub and ad-lib.)

Even bomb threats from an increasingly unstable Healy did not make the Stooges give up on their dream. Still, Moe, Larry, and Shemp could not hold what was happening to Ted Healy against him. They knew he had many problems, and they actually wanted to help him with them. On at least one occasion they tried to sober Healy up after a bad drunken episode so that he would show up for a performance on time, even though the Stooges were not a part of the act. Their efforts saved Healy's job. After this particular episode, Healy begged to rejoin the group. Moe assured him that if Healy did not take a drink for the remainder of his current four-month contract, Moe would consider putting the former group back together. Moe realized the chance he was taking in returning to Healy; the Three Lost Souls were gaining an excellent reputation on the theater circuit, working with a new straight man, Jack Walsh. One review said that "Howard, Fine and Howard have one of the most amusing acts in show business." Rejoining Healy could jeopardize their newfound identity.

Healy kept his promise not to drink, but Shemp, unlike the others, did not trust him. The group signed on as Ted and His Stooges to appear in Shubert's Broadway revue *The Passing Show of 1932*. But when Healy was offered more money by the Balaban & Katz Circuit, he found a loophole in his contract with Shubert and accepted the new, higher paying job. For Shemp, this action was the last straw. He refused to leave the Shubert show, and he refused to work with Healy ever again. After telling Moe about his decision, Shemp left the group and, shortly thereafter, went to Hollywood, where he signed on to star as the fight trainer Knobby Walsh in a series of popular two-reel boxing comedies known as the Joe Palooka movies. He went on to appear in a number of other films without Moe and Larry, including the 1934 film *The Knife of the Party,* in which he attempted Stooge-like humor with new partners, complete with face slaps and eye pokes. The bits were not nearly as successful as the originals.

Moe and Larry had not wanted Shemp to leave their act; they had even restructured their salaries so that Shemp would receive slightly more money than they did. But Shemp simply had had too much of Ted Healy. Shemp's was a decision that would not only alter the lives and careers of the Stooges but would also change the future of film comedy itself.

Moe immediately thought of replacing Shemp with their youngest brother, Jerome. Known as Babe, he was a shy, handsome young man with a waxed mustache and thick, wavy brown hair. His looks and style attracted numerous girlfriends. He had done a little comedy of his own, but mostly he stayed at home with his parents, waiting for the day when his older brothers would let him into their act. For years he watched them closely, learning the routines and imagining himself onstage with them. Although their parents were very much against this idea, it was almost all Babe could think about (except for women). So when Shemp, in 1932, told Babe of his decision to leave the group, which meant that Moe and Larry would need a third Stooge, Babe immediately called Moe. Moe set up an appointment for Babe to meet Healy. But the shy, reserved Babe did not know what to do at his audition and was disappointed when Healy told him that he was too conventionally attractive. With his mustache and thick, wavy hair, he would never fit in with the group. Frustrated and unsure of what to do next, Babe

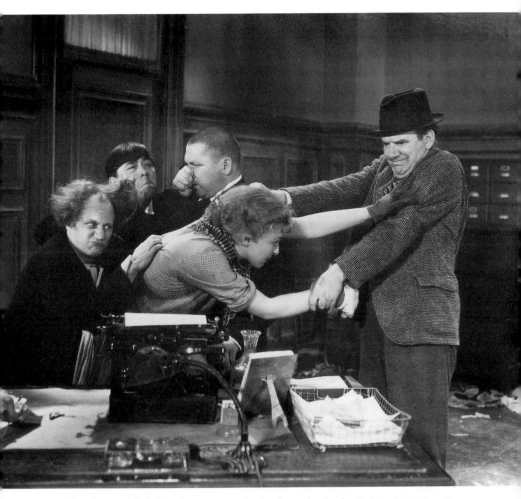

opted for the unthinkable: he went to the barber who had been cutting his beautiful locks for years and told him to shave them all off. The amazed barber made Babe repeat this request several times before he went ahead and made Babe as bald as a cue ball. (He left the mustache, which Babe himself cut off later.)

Babe quickly returned to Healy, a cap pulled firmly over his head. When he removed the cap and revealed his bald pate to Healy and the others, he was immediately welcomed into the group. Moe, Larry, and "Curly"

Ted Healy (right) and Larry, Moe, and Curly appear in *Big Idea,* a film short from the early 1930s. Shemp Howard left the act in 1932 after Moe and Larry decided to rejoin Healy, whom Shemp believed could not be trusted. Curly, the youngest Howard, became the third Stooge.

(he needed a nickname not only because of his new look but because Shemp's wife was also known as Babe) were now a team. But Ted Healy was still in charge of the act.

What happened next belongs in a slapstick film of its own. In 1933, Healy and His Stooges were in the midst of an important series of shows at the Club New Yorker in the Christie Hotel in Hollywood, California. Curly had blended into the group very successfully, and every night his skill in farce just got better and better. At first, his performance consisted of running across the stage carrying a pail of water. After approximately a month of performances, he expanded his repertoire to include dialogue and slapstick—being on the receiving end of Moe and Larry's slaps and pokes. Although offstage he was still very difficult to talk to because of his shyness, onstage he was a comedic force.

The Stooges' appearances at the Club New Yorker were quite popular. Among those with reservations for the Stooges' engagement were important Hollywood residents, including actor Wallace Beery, actress Loretta Young, dancer Ginger Rogers, and producer-director Mervyn Le Roy, who had directed the controversial film *I Am a Fugitive from a Chain Gang* in 1932. After finishing one particularly excellent show, the Stooges were welcomed by thunderous applause that seemed to shake the theater. The group was ecstatic about its overwhelming success in Hollywood until they realized what was really happening: a minor earthquake had struck Los Angeles. After all the excitement and fear had dissipated, a scout from MGM (one of Hollywood's most important movie studios), who had been a member of the audience, signed the group to a one-year deal.

Ted Healy signed the contract on June 3, 1933. He agreed to pay Moe, Larry, and Curly out of his share and to pay for all wardrobe expenses, which of course were minimal. Once again he took the lion's share of the money. The Stooges acceded to the deal because they were happy to be making movies.

Their first film was the 20-minute short *Nertsery Rhymes,* released on July 6, 1933. As an experiment, MGM shot the film in the two-color process, which uses only black, white, red, and green to create an effect that resembles true color. The Stooges played children in the film, waiting to hear bedtime stories. Their second film, released on August 26 of the same year, was *Beer and Pretzels.* In 1990, film critic Leonard Maltin called this film "their best" during the MGM years. The group played a comedy act called Heel-Heely-Heely & Heely ("Ducky Entertainers"), and the film both starts and ends with them being thrown out of the stage door of a nightclub.

MGM also used the group in feature films. In 1933 they appeared in *Meet the Baron,* with comedy stars Jimmy Durante, Zasu Pitts, and others. The *Times-Mirror* wrote that "Ted Healy and His Stooges nearly steal the picture." A month later *Dancing Lady* was released, and this time the group costarred with Joan Crawford, Clark Gable, and Franchot Tone. The executive producer of the film, David O. Selznick, later went on to produce such films as *Gone with the Wind* and *The Third Man.* But Healy still was getting top billing. In *The Big Idea* (1934), Healy's name actually appears above the title:

Ted Healy in *The Big Idea*
 with His Three Stooges
 (Howard, Fine and Howard)

Their last feature film as a group for MGM was in 1934, in *Hollywood Party,* in which they appeared not only with the great comedy team Laurel and Hardy but also with Mickey Mouse.

During this time the Stooges also had cameo parts in other MGM films. In 1934, Curly, billed as Jerry Howard, appeared in *Roast-Beef and Movies*. Moe and Curly played hapless clowns in *Broadway to Hollywood* and con men selling hair tonic in *Jailbirds of Paradise*. (To

In the 1933 MGM film *Dancing Lady,* Curly, Moe, and Larry play a musical number for Joan Crawford and Ted Healy. In addition to shorts, MGM employed the Stooges in feature films, although, according to one critic, the studio "never knew quite what to do with the team."

prove that the hair tonic works, Curly pulls off his wig and proclaims, "Why, six months ago I was as bald as this!") Larry had one line ("Will you play 'Fuzzy Wuzzy'?") in *Stage Mother,* a film that featured Ted Healy in a more substantial role. While all of the Stooges'

In January 1934, waiters Moe, Larry, and Curly serve customer Healy in a swank restaurant. Because Healy considered himself the star of the group despite the praise the Stooges received from reviewers and audiences and because Healy still earned more money than the others, Moe decided the time had come for the Stooges to make it on their own.

individual appearances were in minor, bit parts, Healy was getting much bigger roles on his own. Thus, he still considered himself the star of the group, even though the reviews (which nearly always singled out the Stooges, not Healy) and the audience told a different story.

Even those who do not praise the Stooges' work with MGM recognize the importance of the films. In June 1990, professor and film historian William K. Everson wrote in *Video Review* of the Stooges' MGM years, "It's a period in which the Stooges hadn't really hit their stride, or made a successful transition from a vaudeville style. Still, without being especially funny, the various MGM shorts they made—and their guest appearances in such MGM feature films as *Fugitive Lovers* and *Dancing*

Lady—are fascinating. For one thing, MGM never knew quite what to do with the team. . . . One gets a chance in these early comedies to see the Stooges' slapstick routines as well as their own differing persona undergoing a development and polishing process. In most of this early work, the Stooges were still literally the stooges of Ted Healy." They would not be for long.

While watching one of Healy's solo film appearances, Moe noticed that Healy used many of the same gestures he used when he was with the Stooges onstage, but because the Stooges were not with him, he looked awkward and uncomfortable. The realization that Healy needed the Stooges more than the Stooges needed him, coupled with the Stooges' own growing reputation, led Moe to break away from Healy. Of course, that the Stooges were still being underpaid by Healy no doubt affected Moe's decision. (Different reports show that the Stooges made anywhere from $100 to $150 a week, with some claiming that Moe made more than Larry, and Curly made far less than the other two.)

Healy and Moe parted ways amicably, two longtime friends who had been through a lot together, prepared now to go their separate ways. The gossip columns bemoaned the end of Ted Healy and His Stooges. No one, including Moe, Larry, and Curly themselves, were sure that the Stooges would be able to make it on their own. But then came that fateful day when Moe and Larry, upon leaving MGM separately, signed movie deals. The Three Stooges were off to make films for Columbia; they were ready to take Hollywood by storm.

4 Movie Maniacs

THE TIME HAD COME for Moe, Larry, and Curly to make their first two-reeler for Columbia. The contract they had signed stated that they would make one two-reel short film for the studio, which the studio executives would evaluate for up to 60 days. If the film was successful, Columbia could exercise the option of signing them to a long-term deal. Understandably, the three were nervous, for their whole career in movies rested on the success or failure of this first venture with Columbia, shot in June 1934.

Oddly, the short, called *Woman Haters,* listed Howard, Fine, and Howard separately instead of as a team. Written by the director, Archie Gottler, in rhyme, the musical starred Larry and featured Moe and Curly. It seemed to go well—Columbia liked their performance. Still, as Moe Howard recalls in his memoirs, he was anxious to get the long-term deal signed. He spent two feverish nights and a day writing a nine-page outline of a boxing comedy called *Punch Drunks,* which was based on an idea he had had for some time, then showed it to the studio. A few days later, a Columbia executive named

In a publicity photograph, the private images of Curly, Larry, and Moe have been juxtaposed with their public personas, the characters of the Three Stooges.

Ben Kahane called the three to a meeting. Pleased and impressed by the outline for *Punch Drunks,* Columbia offered them a 7-year contract, renewable at Columbia's discretion each year, for 8 two-reel comedies per year, to be shot over a period of 40 weeks. The remaining 12 weeks of the year belonged to Moe, Larry, and Curly for vaudeville tours, personal appearances, or whatever they wanted to do—except appear in any other film productions. The group's total income from Columbia came to $60,000 per year, a tremendous sum in the depths of the Great Depression. Just a short time earlier, with Ted Healy, they were making about $5,000 each per year. The good life beckoned, and they knew they were about to share their own uproarious slapstick with the world.

Two-reelers were in great demand by movie theaters across the country. Film historians estimate that by the end of the 1930s, two-thirds of all Americans went to the movies every single week. There they were entertained not only by full-length feature films but also by two-reel comedy shorts, newsreels, and cartoons shown before each feature. Prior to television, newsreels were the only source for exciting moving pictures of the rest of the world, and cartoons and two-reelers filled the need for light entertainment today provided by situation comedies and Saturday morning animated shows. Successful comedians could be seen by a nationwide audience nearly every week. The Stooges knew that with hard work, luck, and determination they could become household names. The work would indeed be hard.

Billed officially as the Three Stooges at last, in June 1934, Moe, Larry, and Curly plunged into the maelstrom of their busy studio shooting schedule. Completing 8 two-reelers in 40 weeks meant about 5 weeks for each short, and often even less time than that. Their physical, sometimes brutal slapstick ensured plenty of mishaps and various injuries for all. The Stooges did their own stunts,

In this Columbia film, managers Moe and Larry twist wrestler Curly's ears as he holds an opponent in a neck grip during a match. Columbia offered the Stooges a seven-year contract and a total of $60,000 per year for their slapstick.

and their days in vaudeville served them well, for there they had learned how to do eye pokes and head bops relatively safely. (The key to the eye pokes was that Moe poked extremely quickly, just below the eyebrows. The violence of the head bops was due to similar sleight of hand and clever sound effects.) Still, they all later recalled more than a few injuries.

In *Punch Drunks* (1934), the plot that Moe wrote called for Curly to burst into a punching fury whenever Larry played "Pop Goes the Weasel" on his violin. Moe portrayed Curly's boxing manager. For some of the fight scenes, a professional boxer sparred in the ring with Curly, who wound up with a real bloody nose and lip. The climactic scene occurs when Larry's violin breaks during a bout and he must madly search for something to inspire the now peaceful Curly. He finds and steals a

49

truck with a loudspeaker over which is played "Pop Goes the Weasel." The actor who somersaults from the back of the truck actually broke his arm when he rolled off the truck.

The Stooges' next short was a parody of *Men in White*, a 1934 hospital drama starring Clark Gable, who went on to play Rhett Butler in *Gone with the Wind*. In the Stooges' version, called *Men in Black* (1934), the Stooges played three zany interns. It featured an entirely ad-libbed scene in which the three addressed their surgical instruments with hilariously crazy made-up terms. The film was their only one ever to be nominated for an Academy Award for best short.

Three Little Pigskins (1934), a football movie, followed. A young Lucille Ball, who achieved stardom in the 1950s in the *I Love Lucy* television series, appeared as

In *Three Little Pigskins* (1934), the Three Stooges actually played football with the Loyola University football team; six actors ended up in the hospital when they broke bones filming one scene.

Daisy Simms, the girlfriend of a gangster. In later years Ball claimed, "The only thing I ever learned from [the Stooges] was how to duck." Others in the production evidently did not learn how to duck quite as well as Ball. Moe recalled that after one scene featuring actors and actual Loyola University football players, six actors wound up in the hospital with broken bones.

The following year the Stooges made seven shorts. Among them was *Pop Goes the Easel,* notable in that it is the first time they were teamed with director Del Lord, who went on to direct many of their most successful shorts. Also, the two girls playing hopscotch in one of the scenes are none other than Joan Howard, Moe's daughter, and Phyllis Fine, Larry's daughter, the only time they appeared in any of their fathers' films.

In late 1935 and early 1936, the Stooges began their longtime association with Jules White, whose first film as producer for the group was *Movie Maniacs* (1936). White, who was head of the Columbia short subjects department, continued to direct and produce shorts for the Stooges for the next 23 years.

Throughout the next decade Moe, Larry, and Curly kept up a busy filming schedule. Their former partner, Ted Healy, was not so lucky. His career ended sadly, as he was killed in a nightclub brawl in 1937. By the end of 1939, Columbia had released 43 two-reel Three Stooges shorts. The boys also appeared in two feature films: in bit parts as musicians in *The Captain Hates the Sea* in 1934, and as firemen in *Start Cheering* in 1938. In both films the Stooges crossed paths with Hollywood legends. *The Captain Hates the Sea* starred John Gilbert in his last film role. He had been the romantic idol of the silent screen, adored by millions, just a few years earlier. *Start Cheering* featured the popular entertainer Jimmy Durante.

The Three Stooges comedies also starred a number of talented supporting players. One favorite theme for the

The Three Stooges (front row, right) appeared in *Start Cheering* with entertainer Jimmy "Da Schnozz" Durante in 1938. Larry, Moe, and Curly played firemen in the Columbia feature film.

shorts involved casting the Stooges as lowly workers who somehow are called upon to impersonate members of high society or to mingle with them. Some of their most beloved mayhem occurs in these comedies, which include *Pardon My Scotch* and *Hoi Polloi* (1935), *Ants in the Pantry* and *Slippery Silks* (1936), and *Termites of 1938*. In many, an actress named Symona Boniface plays a high-class guest or society matron on the receiving end of pies and cream puffs hurled by the Stooges. A distinguished, hardworking actress, she came from a well-known

theatrical family from the Northeast. William Bletcher, who appeared in *Punch Drunks* and *Pardon My Scotch,* had a long career as a vaudevillian and later as a voice-over artist in commercials and Disney animated shorts. His last role was a guest appearance on the television show "Charlie's Angels" in 1978.

The Stooges kept busy making shorts and working with the wide assortment of lesser-known actors who formed the backbone of Hollywood in those days. *Disorder in the Court,* an all-time favorite of many fans, was released in 1936. Today the film is regularly shown on the American Movie Classics (AMC) cable television station, which features classic films from the glory days of Hollywood, the 1930s, 1940s, and 1950s. Thus, it is possible to catch Larry accidentally pulling off a court officer's toupee with his violin bow and screaming that it is a tarantula, Curly pounding Moe's foot trying to kill it, and Moe ultimately shooting it, in between films by such directors as Alfred Hitchcock, Frank Capra, and John Huston.

Disorder in the Court features a number of classic Stooges routines, including a wonderful swearing-in scene with Curly and a court officer. In the bit, Curly wears a bowler hat and holds a cane. The court officer tells Curly to place his right hand in the air and put his left hand on the Bible. He starts to do so, but the judge tells him to take off his hat. Curly removes his hat, but with neither hand now free (his other hand is holding the cane), he has to put his hat back on his head so he can put his left hand on the Bible as he switches his cane from his left hand to his right, which he then raises into the air. The judge yells at him to take off his hat, forcing Curly to put the cane back in his left hand and his hat in his right. With both the court officer and the judge yelling at him, a frustrated Curly raises his right hand with the cane in it, the bowler resting on the hook of the cane. After continuing back and forth, Curly finally places the hat on the court officer's head, hooks the cane onto the officer's arm, and tells him to raise *his* right hand. Eventually Curly is sworn in and told to take the stand. At that point, Curly feels he has no choice but to ask the frustrated judge where he wants it.

Disorder in the Court, in a way, sums up Curly's (and the Stooges') appeal. The repetitious dialogue is typical of their routines—witty wordplay did not have a large role in their comedy, although silly puns form the title of many of their shorts: for example, *Three Little Sew and Sews* (1939), *No Census, No Feeling* (1940), and *Cactus Makes Perfect* (1942). Their talents lay not in repartee but in physical comedy—their facial expressions, their body motions, and their gestures, all of which are used to maximum visual effect. Describing Curly's consternation during the swearing-in scene cannot make one laugh, but seeing his rotund face squinched up in confusion can. During the late 1930s and early 1940s, the Stooges developed and refined physical gags that they would continue to use in film for years to come.

Each stooge had a repertoire of characteristic gestures. Moe was a bully, squashing hapless Curly's head in a vise. Crazy Larry contributed absurd suggestions, which were greeted by Moe's cry "You knuckleheads!" Some of Curly's most famous antics included continually flapping his hands over his face in frustration, answering silly questions with "soitenly," and doing the wild Curly dance, in which he would twist, twirl, go backward, roll on the floor, and smooth his bald head. Larry's was usually a befuddled expression beneath his insanely frizzled hair—which was often pulled out by Moe as he slammed together Larry and Curly's heads.

Still, the Stooges had lives offscreen, and their own dynamics as a group and as individuals matured. Moe emerged as the leader of the group onscreen and off. After Larry's attempt to sign with Universal in 1934, he never concerned himself with the Stooges' financial or legal matters. Their business affairs were ably handled by Moe.

Devoted to his wife, Helen, and his children, Joan and Paul, Moe happily ignored the glittering lifestyle of Hollywood and concentrated on securing the group's financial success and making his family happy. Ed Bernds, one of the Stooges' longtime directors, recalled Moe as extremely hardworking and "all business." His daughter,

Joan, her husband, Norman Maurer, and other friends have recounted stories of Moe's generosity and kindness. Once, on the spur of the moment, he bought Christmas groceries for longtime Stooges sidekick Emil Sitka and his whole family, which included seven people. He volunteered his services to a society that helped children who had cerebral palsy (impaired muscular power and coordination from brain damage usually incurred before or at birth) and served as its president three times.

Larry Fine and his wife, Mabel, disliked housekeeping and lived in hotels in Atlantic City, New Jersey, and Hollywood, California, with their two children, Phyllis and Johnny. They enjoyed entertaining fellow actors and actresses at extravagant parties, where Larry could keep the guests laughing. Although Larry was a talented comedian, his suggestions for gags for the Stooges' routines were mostly ignored, for many people did not understand his offbeat sense of humor. Still, he never became upset about being passed over. Emil Sitka described Larry as "a happy-go-lucky guy that was always eager for the scene to finish so he could go off to the races." He and Mabel were favorite guests and hosts in the Hollywood community. One area in which Larry was not skillful, however, was managing his money. In fact, in his later years he said, "Moe saved his money—I spent mine."

Moe's youngest brother, Curly, who had always lived for the moment, could barely be restrained from spending his paycheck as soon as he got it. He loved cars, pretty women, and all the accoutrements of a Hollywood star. In 1937 he married Elaine Ackerman, and they had a daughter, Marilyn, but the marriage failed four years later. It was his second marriage; his first, in the late 1920s, had been dissolved at his mother's insistence. Even then, he preferred to spend time dancing and drinking in nightclubs, entertaining his friends by playing the spoons, or ripping up tablecloths in time to the music.

Years later Elaine said, "He was a real cutup when we were out in public."

In fact, Curly's mother, Jennie, had taken him to Europe immediately after she broke up his first marriage. On his own for a time, he enjoyed himself vastly with the amusements offered by Paris, France, in the roaring 1920s. Ten years later, nothing had changed. Throughout the 1930s and early 1940s, Curly's lifestyle remained wild offscreen, though he is remembered by many as shy, good-hearted, and sometimes almost morose. Actress Julie Gibson, who had to kiss Curly in *Three Smart Saps* (1942), said of him, "He was so painfully shy that he really did not know how to communicate with you. So the minute they said cut, poor Curly just disappeared into the woodwork." He suffered terribly in self-esteem as a result of his shaven head. Paradoxically, his bald pate made him a success onscreen and miserable when away from the cameras.

Despite their differing lifestyles, the trio worked well together. When not hectically filming for Columbia, they made appearances in person—paid, of course. In fact, much of their income came from the 12 weeks a year they spent appearing onstage in New York, Boston, and other big cities. Their fame grew through their film work, and they became even more popular and successful as live performers.

In 1939, they were invited to perform in London, England, at the renowned Palladium. They traveled overseas on the prestigious *Queen Mary* ocean liner. The captain was so impressed with their fame that he transferred them to first class for free. Moe recalled one of the headlines in the London newspapers: STOOGES ARRIVE IN LONDON—QUEEN LEAVES FOR AMERICA. The trio was touched by the affection shown them overseas. They appeared in extended engagements in London; in Blackpool, England; and in Dublin, Ireland, where a crowd of admirers made off with Curly's hat and tore the pockets off his coat in a frenzy of admiration. In Dublin, the impresario presenting them told the boys that he had to change their name on the marquee to "The Three Hooges" because in the Irish slang of that time, "to stooge" meant to have sexual intercourse. They made a great splash in Dublin and proceeded on to Glasgow, Scotland. They returned to the United States in the middle of 1939, once again on the *Queen Mary*. Moe remembered it was the last time the great liner crossed the Atlantic Ocean during peacetime. World War II was about to begin.

The Three Stooges had to return to America not because of the war but because they were booked to appear on Broadway in New York, in the *George White Scandals of 1939*. The show (which was not scandalous at all) featured a number of comedy sketches, tap dancers, and singers. It was hugely successful, and during its run a fabulous sign displaying the Stooges' eye-poking routine in sparkling moving lights adorned Broadway. The trio returned to California just before the end of the show's run to resume their film work for Columbia.

Despite the light content of the Stooges' shorts, one short from 1940 stands apart from the others. *You Nazty Spy* has been singled out in the *Three Stooges Journal*, by Don B. Moran of the University of Dayton in Ohio, as the first American comedy release to ridicule German dictator Adolf Hitler. Shot in just seven days, the film preceded Charlie Chaplin's *The Great Dictator* (in which the Little Tramp gets mistaken for Adolf Hitler with hilarious—and very serious—results) by nine months. Moe plays Moe Hailstone, and references to Hitler throughout the film are unmistakable. All of the Stooges' families had fled anti-Semitic persecution in Europe, and in a small way their work in this film helped bring the Nazi threat to the forefront of moviegoers' attention. At

You Nazty Spy was released to theaters on January 19, 1940, nine months before Charlie Chaplin's movie *The Great Dictator*. Moe Howard was the first film actor to deride the German dictator Adolf Hitler—at a time when most Americans supported an isolationist view regarding the war in Europe.

the time the public seemed averse to any reference to political events overseas. Just prior to World War II, the last subject Americans wanted to think about was foreign affairs. A popular political movement known as isolationism held that U.S. interests were best served by avoiding involvement in other countries' affairs and concentrating on America's own problems. In spite of the public's fear of becoming involved in foreign nations' conflicts, the Stooges' short was successful, making money for Columbia.

Throughout the early 1940s the Three Stooges continued making Columbia shorts, including *A-Plumbing We Will Go* (1940), *All the World's a Stooge* (1941), *Loco Boys Make Good* (1942), and numerous others. Many fans feel these are some of their greatest short films. Throughout, Curly was a mainspring of humor. When he could

Jerome "Curly" Howard nyuk-nyuks the camera in this Columbia movie still. On-screen, Curly was a gifted comedian; offscreen, he had severe marital and health problems.

not remember his lines, he would throw in a perfectly timed "nyuk-nyuk-nyuk" or "woo-woo-woo." On-screen he was a comedy genius. Offscreen, his life was not nearly as funny.

Moe had bought a lovely home in To-luca Lake, California, where he gardened, cooked for his and his wife's friends, and relaxed with his adored children. Curly was divorced from Elaine Ackerman in 1941 and invited various family members to share his home. Despite having his caring relatives around him, Curly became very depressed and lived like a recluse. During the early 1940s, Moe became worried about Curly and his lonely lifestyle. By 1945, Curly's health had become so bad—from drinking too much, overeating, and keeping terrible hours—that he began missing cues, unable to perform to the best of his ability. Moe introduced a pretty young woman, Marion Buchsbaum, to his youngest brother, sure that a happy home life like his own could settle Curly down. After a whirlwind courtship, Marion and Curly were married on October 17, 1945. Unfortunately, the pair proved a poor match. They were separated in January 1946, and Marion criticized Curly in the popular press. A *Los Angeles Times* article on June 6, 1946, aired some of their dirty laundry in public, with both sides making nasty allegations about the other. The article claimed that Marion had agreed to marry Curly only after "he had given her $250 for clothes, a $3750 mink coat and an $850 wrist watch." It was obviously a very ugly, very public divorce.

After the divorce decree, Curly's health began to deteriorate even more rapidly. It is believed that through 1945 and 1946, Curly suffered a series of minor strokes without telling anyone about them. It is possible that he did not recognize some of them himself, brushing them off as hangovers from his excessive drinking. However, his performances in the Stooges films were suffering as a result of his ill health. He was no longer able to do many of the wonderful bits, such as spinning like a top on the floor, for which he was famous; he even had more trouble than ever remembering his lines.

While filming *Half-Wit's Holiday* in 1946, Curly suffered a debilitating stroke on the set. Upon seeing his youngest brother slumped helplessly in director Jules White's chair, Moe broke down in tears. The team had made 97 shorts for Columbia, but it looked as if the days of Howard, Fine, and Howard were now over. Curly went to the Motion Picture Country Home and Hospital (now known as the Motion Picture & Television Country House & Hospital) in Calabassas, California to recuperate, but he would appear only once more with his brother Moe and friend Larry, in a cameo in *Hold That Lion.* The rest of his life was spent with his fourth wife, Valerie, whom he married in 1947, and their daughter, Jane. He was happily retired, although he suffered a number of other small strokes and was not in good health.

Moe had been upset after Curly's major stroke. Larry had donated some of his salary to help pay for Curly's medical expenses. Despite their profound sorrow over Curly's retirement, Moe was determined that the Three Stooges would carry on. But who could be the third Stooge? The answer was not very far away at all. Once again, Moe and Larry turned to the Howard family for their solution.

61

5 Gents in a Jam

CURLY'S RETIREMENT and diminished capacities had saddened Moe greatly. Curly had been the baby of the family, had idolized his older brothers, and had been his mother's favorite. Moe felt for his brother and for his personal problems and ill health. He also knew how important Curly's inspired clowning had been to the Stooges. Although Larry was not a Howard brother, he understood how close the Howards were to each other and realized that a phase of the Stooges' career had ended forever; never again would the trio perform quite the same act. Moe gave the question of Curly's replacement much thought. He decided he wanted his brother Shemp Howard to become the third Stooge. Larry suggested that each of the Stooges contribute $50 a week to give to Curly, and the other two agreed. They were a team again. Initially, Columbia executives rejected Moe's suggestion because they thought Shemp looked too much like Moe, but they relented. Shemp once again was a Stooge.

Shemp was walking into a very difficult situation. He had to take the place of one of the most beloved figures in movie comedy. There was little doubt

---

In *A-Plumbing We Will Go,* a 1940 short, plumber Curly entraps himself in pipes while trying to fix a leak. Curly suffered a major stroke and died on January 18, 1952.

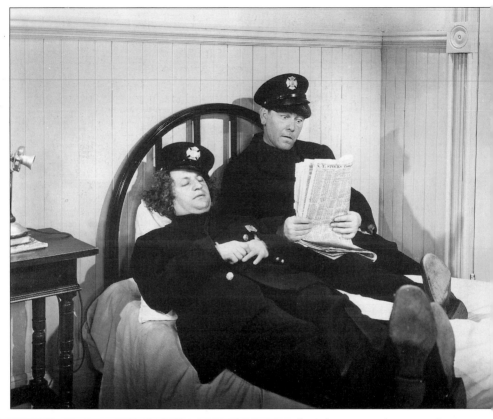

Fireman Larry catches 40 winks as fireman Moe scrutinizes a newspaper article in a scene from one of their films. After Curly suffered a debilitating stroke, Larry and Moe asked Moe's brother Shemp if he would rejoin the Stooges.

that Shemp would fit in well with Moe and Larry; after all, he had been one of the original stooges with Ted Healy's act. But the public loved Curly, and it was impossible to know how the audiences would react to his replacement, even if it was Curly's own brother Shemp. As veteran Stooges director Edward Bernds recalled, "Comparing [Shemp] to Curly is not fair. He could never be Curly and never tried to be. . . . The transition, as far as I was concerned, was all for the good."

After leaving the Stooges in 1932, Shemp had embarked on a successful career in Hollywood. He had worked and starred in a number of comedy shorts series, including the Joe Palooka Series, the Andy Clyde Series, and the Shemp Howard Series. The Clyde and Howard series were written, directed, and produced by Jules White, Felix Adler, Edward Bernds, Del Lord, and Elwood Ullman, who were all making Three Stooges shorts with Moe, Larry, and Curly at the time as well. Among the feature films Shemp had appeared in were *The Bank Dick* (1940), with W. C. Fields; *Buck Privates* (1940), *In the Navy*, and *Hold That Ghost* (both released in 1941) with Bud Abbott and Lou Costello; and *Hit the Road* (also released in 1941), with the Dead End Kids, later known as the Bowery Boys.

Shemp and his wife, Gertrude, enjoyed their life and their home in North Hollywood. The guest lists at their many intimate parties included some of the great comedians of the time, including Phil Silvers (who gained fame on television as Sergeant Bilko in the 1950s program "You'll Never Get Rich," later renamed "The Phil Silvers Show") and Martha Raye, a singer and comedian known for her wide mouth and good lungs. Although the parties would stop when one contract expired, they would begin again when the next one was signed. Shemp's niece Dolly Sallin recalled that "Shemp was really a quiet, family man who had evening get-togethers where friends would drop in. He was quite devoted to his wife and son [Mort]." Shemp's nephew Norman Maurer (Moe's son-in-law) remembers Shemp as "a delightful man. He was the funniest of the three brothers . . . he was a riot."

Shemp gained a reputation not only for his funny, likable personal qualities but also for his many phobias. He had a fear of water, driving (and cars), airplanes, and dogs. (His fear of dogs is ironic, considering his brother Curly's tremendous love of them.) Whenever he had to play a scene with an animal or with water, he became nervous and frightened. When he appeared with Joe Besser in a scene from the 1949 Abbott and Costello film *Africa Screams,* the cast and crew mischievously teased

Shemp because he was afraid to get on a raft in water that was only about two feet deep.

Shemp's first role with the Three Stooges was in *Fright Night,* released on March 6, 1947. The part he played, that of one of three managers of boxer Chopper Kane (Moe and Larry played the other two managers), had originally been written for Curly, but Shemp smoothly stepped right in. The lobby card for the short claimed, "The Stooges'll have *you* hangin' on the ropes . . . with laughter!" and gives Shemp top billing above his two partners. Shemp considered the film his personal favorite among all the Stooges films he appeared in not only because it was his first with the group but also because it was about boxing, a sport he ardently admired.

The third film made by Moe, Larry, and Shemp was the 100th short in the career of the Three Stooges at Columbia. *Hold That Lion,* released in July 1947, was also the only short to include Moe, Larry, Shemp—and Curly. In an unscripted cameo, Curly appears as a train passenger whom the Stooges bump into while trying to catch a con artist. Curly is actually somewhat disguised in the scene, sporting a full head of hair under his bowler hat and a clothespin clamped onto his nose, which distorts most of his face. Sadly, it was Curly's last film appearance, for his strokes had disabled him so much that he could no longer work.

Shemp's style was very different from Curly's. Whereas Curly had his "woo-woo-woos" and "nyuk-nyuk-nyuks," Shemp had his high-pitched "heep-heep-heeps." Curly spun around and around on the floor, did various hysterical dances and hilarious walks, and made extremely funny and charming faces. Shemp had his head shoved through walls, got beaten up constantly (by women, usually), and was interminably pushing his long, stringy hair out of his rough, chiseled, and decidedly unhandsome face.

Emil Sitka, whose first appearance in a Stooges film was in Curly's last short, *Half-Wit's Holiday* (1947), became one of the Stooges' most popular supporting actors throughout the Shemp years. He believed that "Shemp was the funniest of them all." In describing a typical day on the set, Sitka said, "A lot of people think it might have been like a circus. It was more like an operating room. . . . Believe it or not, the Stooges were real professionals." Jock Mahoney, a Stooges supporting actor and stuntman who later played Tarzan in features, said of making Stooges films, "It was like choreographing a dance." As crazy as their antics were while the camera was on, off camera they were very serious about their work, especially Moe, who would work with

Shemp prepares to throw cake at Larry while Moe threatens to force-feed Larry with a fork. Although Shemp had been a Stooge during the early days with Healy, he realized that Curly, one of the most popular characters in comedy, was a tough act to follow.

the writer and director on both the script and the structure of the film.

On January 18, 1952, Moe received the long-dreaded news that his beloved brother Curly had died. For a few years at the end of the 1940s, Curly had lived peacefully in retirement with his wife Valerie, daughter Janie, and dog Lady, but by 1950 he was confined to a wheelchair. By 1951 his worsening condition necessitated a move to the North Hollywood Hospital and Sanitarium, and he remained hospitalized for the rest of his life. He spent his last month at the Baldy View Sanitarium in San Gabriel, California, where he died, at the age of 48, leaving behind his wife, 3-year-old Jane, and 11-year-old Marilyn (his daughter with Elaine Ackerman). Moe and Shemp were saddened but realized that at last Curly's years of suffering had ended.

Bud Abbott (right) and Lou Costello are seen here in the 1942 movie comedy *Who Done It?* After Shemp left the Stooges in 1932, he acted in numerous comedy shorts and feature films, including three movies with the popular comedy team Abbott and Costello.

From 1947 to 1952, Larry, Moe, and Shemp made 44 films together. Among them were *Brideless Groom* (1947), *Squareheads of the Round Table* (1948), *Punchy Cowpunchers* (1950), *Scrambled Brains* (1951), and *Corny Casanovas* (1952). After *Gents in a Jam,* which was released on July 4, 1952, another major upheaval occurred in the professional world of the Stooges. Producer Hugh McCollum and writer-director Ed Bernds left Columbia to work with another popular comedy team, the Bowery Boys. Writer Elwood Ullman had left a few films earlier to go into television. (Ullman did, however, receive writing credit in a number of later Stooges films because the films were remakes of or included stock footage from previous films that he had scripted.) Thus, one of the Stooges' great behind-the-scenes teams broke up. Jules White took control as producer-director.

Whereas Bernds allowed improvisation (Shemp was especially proficient at ad-libbing), White was more dictatorial. Emil Sitka said Bernds was an "entirely different director, [with an] entirely different approach. He allowed me to create the character." White preferred to stick more to the script and have the characters develop the way he wanted them to. The team of producer-director Jules White, director Del Lord, and writers Felix Adler and Jack White (Jules's brother) combined to make the next 29 Stooges shorts with Shemp, Larry, and Moe. The regular crew of Columbia supporting actors appeared as well, including Sitka, Boniface, and Christine McIntyre. Among these films were *Spooks* and *Pardon My Backfire* (both released in 1953), two attempts at capturing the lunacy of the Stooges in three-dimensional (3-D) film, a fad at the time. (Although many people have claimed that *Pardon My Backfire* was not filmed in 3-D, it was shown in that format at the Seventh Annual Three Stooges Convention in July 1993.) Even though the 3-D films were not particularly successful, the Stooges remained as popular as ever. Every year between 1950 and 1955, they received the Laurel Award, presented annually by film exhibitors to the year's top money-making shorts.

Times were changing, however, and comedians could make money in a whole new field: television. In the early 1950s, television began the home entertainment revolution. Fewer Americans went out to the weekly movie; instead, families and friends gathered around their fascinating new television sets to watch their favorite weekly shows. During this period the Stooges continued their relentless schedule of live performances and added television appearances as well. They first appeared on the new medium on October 19, 1948, on Milton Berle's "Texaco Star Theater." Berle was perhaps the most famous entertainer on the small screen. America adopted him as Uncle Miltie; he was also known as Mister Television. Tuesday night in America was Uncle Miltie night.

In the early years of television, most programs were shown live, unlike contemporary times when nearly every show is filmed or taped. Filming and taping allow actors and directors to do scenes over and over again until they are right. Live television allows no mistakes; a missed line or cue is glaringly obvious and is seen by millions of people. At first the Stooges were uncomfortable with the fast-paced nature of live television. Although they had performed live onstage, their acting for television would be very different. Because of TV's shooting schedule, very little rehearsal time was available. The Stooges often resorted to doing older routines from their stage shows and films, routines they knew by heart.

They did, however, take a stab at their own weekly show in October 1949, featuring mostly new routines. The pilot, or trial show, was filmed in front of a live audience. The show, called simply "The Three Stooges," was produced by Phil Berle, Milton's brother. The trio portrayed painters and paper hangers; as usual, they were

working-class characters. A sign shown at the beginning of the program identifies some of their other occupations: Fizzicians, Soigeons, Uptometrists, and Downtownetrists. The first episode, entitled "Fools of the Trade," costarred Stooges regulars Emil Sitka and Symona Boniface as Mr. and Mrs. Pennyfeather. It was the usual Stooges humor, filled with sight gags, including a file cabinet whose drawers open on Stooges heads, a food fight, and an uproarious gag involving a pressure cooker salesman from Punxatawney, Pennsylvania. At one point

The Three Stooges dance a routine with their director, Jules White (standing, center), in a scene from one of their shorts. White, head of Columbia's short-subjects department, was known among the film crew as the Fourth Stooge because he often raised his voice on the set while directing.

Moe asks Larry, "How'd you ever get so stupid?" Larry answers, "I got a charge account. What's your excuse?" One detail that is immediately evident in viewing the show is the lack of sound effects. Their television appearances did not include the bops, pows, and other bizarre noises that accompany the slapping, bumping, and poking of the films, and without them, the skits are not quite as funny. Although the audience loved them, their chance at immediate television stardom quickly ended. Columbia executives, sensing that a television series similar to the Stooges' two-reelers could directly compete with Columbia's product, refused to allow the trio to make or sell the series because of contractual obligations.

The Stooges, however, were still allowed to make guest appearances. One such appearance was on Ed Wynn's "Camel Comedy Caravan" on March 11, 1950, in which Moe taught Wynn how to give a "double zinger" to Shemp and Larry, hitting both with simultaneous eye pokes. They appeared throughout the show, driving Wynn crazy. They eventually cut up the scenery—literally—and even sang. They continued to appear on the Milton Berle show, performing many of their notorious bits from their films as well as brand-new sketches. Berle was a great fan of the Three Stooges. Larry said that "Berle was kind of like [Ted] Healy. He was fast with the jokes and would slap us around. We got into all kinds of messes, of course. And Milton liked having us on the show."

In 1951, the Three Stooges starred in their first full-length feature film. Finally, they received absolutely top billing. Made for United Artists, *Gold Raiders* (also known as *The Stooges Go West*) was written by Ullman and directed by Bernds. Bernds said of the film, "I should never have made that picture." It was shot quickly and cheaply, and, according to Bernds, "the picture shows it."

The Stooges would not make another feature film for eight years.

As successful as the shorts with Shemp were, more and more of their films in 1955 and 1956 were reworkings of earlier shorts. They featured many old gags and even included stock footage from previously released shorts. Whether the team was running dry of new ideas will never be known, for on November 22, 1955, Shemp died of a heart attack in the back of a cab after celebrating at the racetrack and at the fights. According to Moe's memoirs, Shemp had been lively at the fights that night, wildly pretending that he was in the ring. He was putting on a show, and the audience loved it—except for those sitting around him who occasionally caught a jab or two. Riding home in a cab, with a cigar in his mouth, the 60-year-old slumped over onto his friend Al Winston and died, according to Moe, "with a smile on his face." Given his tremendous fear of cars, it was somewhat of an ironic ending for the brilliant, gentle comedian.

For Crimin' Out Loud, Shemp's 73rd film as a member of the Three Stooges, was the last one that featured new footage. Four films followed in 1956, made up of old footage of Shemp combined with new footage of a double, Joe Palma. Another chapter in the life and career of the Howards and the Three Stooges had come to an end. For Moe, the effect was devastating. He had not only lost another partner but another brother as well. The films that Moe and Larry made first with Curly and then with Shemp were extraordinary, in number and creativity. They released 174 two-reelers for Columbia from 1934 to 1956, in addition to the earlier films made with Ted Healy. They had become international stars and were beloved by the American public. Once again disaster had struck, but once more Moe and Larry were determined to go on.

6 A Merry Mix-Up

SHEMP'S DEATH was a crushing blow for Moe and Larry. Moe lost a second brother; Larry lost a close friend and a companion in mayhem. Hollywood gossips wrote that Moe considered breaking up the group, but Columbia held them to their contract, which demanded two more years of two-reel shorts. Moe briefly considered the concept of the Two Stooges, but in the end he suggested a replacement, a well-known Hollywood comedian and longtime acquaintance, Joe Besser.

Joe's career and background had interesting parallels and intersections with those of Moe and Larry. He was born on August 12, 1907. Like the Howards, he was the son of hardworking Eastern European Jewish immigrants. His parents settled in St. Louis, Missouri, where young Joe paid more attention to the movies and to vaudeville shows than to school, just as Moe, Curly, and Shemp had in Brooklyn during their childhood. As soon as Joe finished sixth grade, he got started in show business, quickly finding his way to the vaudeville circuit.

Joe Besser, Moe Howard, and Larry Fine appear in *The Three Stooges Fun-O-Rama*, which was released in 1959. Besser had a successful career in his own comedy series at Columbia Pictures when he joined the Stooges in 1956 as the third Stooge.

His and the Stooges' path first crossed in the J. J. Shubert review *The Passing Show of 1932.* In his autobiography *Not Just a Stooge,* Besser recalled that Ted Healy and his Racketeers headlined the show and that "we became good friends. Having them around was a laugh a minute." Throughout the following years, Joe worked successfully in vaudeville and radio, developing his trademark lines "Not so f-a-a-a-st!" and "You crazy, you!" (These lines were copied by many other performers and appear in the mouths of animated characters in Warner Bros. cartoons of the 1940s, such as "Holiday Steps Out," and even in more recent cartoons such as "Bobby's World.") He worked in a number of Columbia shorts, including *Waiting in the Lurch* (1949), *Dizzy Yardbirds* (1950), *Caught on the Bounce* (1952), and *The Fire Chaser* (1954), with Jules and Jack White, Felix Adler, Ed Bernds, Elwood Ullman, Emil Sitka, and Joe Palma—all Stooges regulars.

Between 1940 and 1955, Besser worked alongside many performers who became the backbone of Hollywood and television. He appeared in 14 feature films, including *The Desert Hawk* (1950). In that film he worked closely with comedy great Jackie Gleason (later star of "The Honeymooners"); the two roly-poly comedians spent most of the time they were not filming playing practical jokes on each other. The film was directed by Frederick De Cordova (who later went on to produce Johnny Carson's "Tonight Show") and included Yvonne De Carlo (who later played Lily, the wife and mother on the hit television series "The Munsters"), George Macready, and young Rock Hudson.

Joe Besser and Lou Costello had been very close friends for years, and Joe worked with Abbott and Costello on several feature films. In 1952, he brought his favorite characterization, that of a feisty, somewhat bratty little kid, to television, where he created the character Stinky for the weekly television series "The Abbott and Costello Show." As Stinky, Besser immortalized the whining line "I'm going to give you such a p-i-i-i-nch!"

Joe had worked with Shemp in the feature *Africa Screams,* and even before that, Joe and his wife, Ernie, socialized with Shemp and Gertrude a great deal, dining at each other's houses regularly. Joe had grieved over his friend's sudden death. When Moe approached him to take Shemp's place, Joe was pleased to accept. However, Besser signed a separate contract with Columbia, on January 1, 1956, calling for him to make $3,500 a week, $1,000 more than Larry and Moe earned.

His comedic credentials were impeccable, and he brought a fresh new approach to the group's work. His childish character talked back and stood up for himself, with hilarious results. Though he had worked in vaudeville, he had not specialized in physical, slapstick humor and was much less comfortable with it than the other two Stooges were. Jules White relied heavily on violent humor, even more than slapstick, and some ob-servers feel his Stooges films with Besser do not work as well as those with Curly and Shemp. Joe refused to be on the receiving end of too many blows or slaps, in part because he did not feel it worked with his character. He recalled: "[Moe and Larry] . . . realized that my character was unlike Curly's and Shemp's and so they treated me like an individual. . . . 'Don't worry, Joe,' said Larry. 'If you don't want Moe to hit you, I'll take all the belts.'"

In a 1983 interview with biographer David N. Brus-kin, Jules White commented, "In Joe Besser, you had the same character function as Curly. They'd both threaten Moe and then back off when he called their challenge. Shemp, on the other hand, was really a comedy villain. You could slap him with a cake or a pie or a bucket of mud because he was such a meanie." When Bruskin asked

Joe Besser tries to prevent Moe from shutting a refrigerator door on Larry. Besser was the only Stooge to defend himself against Moe's constant lambasting.

White whether he had tried to develop a new image for the Three Stooges, White replied:

> I discovered one thing. No matter what you did with these people, no matter what kind of program you made up for them, they were, in the end, the Three Stooges—with Curly, with Shemp, or with Joe Besser. . . . You could not make Joe Besser be Curly. It's a fact. You could try, but

you didn't want him to be Curly. You wanted him to be Joe Besser and fit in with the Three Stooges. He had his own little book of tricks and he was a very cute little character.

The Three Stooges got along well. Joe remembered Larry fondly, referring to him as "a social butterfly. . . . Ernie and I visited Larry and his wife Mabel at their beautiful Griffith Park home several times and Larry always kept us entertained. . . . Larry was a doll!" He did not socialize with Moe, though the two were friendly. Moe always kept away from the Hollywood social scene, whereas Larry and Joe were very much a part of it.

Every year, the Three Stooges made their usual eight shorts for Columbia. Throughout 1957 and 1958, Jules White produced and directed all 16; his brother Jack or Felix Adler wrote most. Harold White, Jules White's oldest son, was the film editor on the first Stooges short with Joe, *Hoofs and Goofs,* as well as three more. Emil Sitka continued his vital supporting roles. The films included *A Merry Mix-Up* (1957), which featured the Stooges playing three pairs of identical triplets, and *Rusty Romeos* (1957), a remake of *Corny Casanovas.* Three of their films gave a nod to the newly popular science-fiction genre: *Space Ship Sappy* (1957), *Outer Space Jitters* (1957) (with Dan Blocker as a monster; Blocker later rose to fame as Hoss on the television series "Bonanza"), and *Flying Saucer Daffy* (1958), which Joe particularly liked. On the other hand, he recalled the musical short *Sweet and Hot* (1958) as "the film I hate the most . . . a dog."

Although the schedule, as usual, was hectic and the personnel remained much the same, the film industry was changing drastically. At the time, Columbia, still under Harry Cohn, was the only studio that continued to operate a short-film division. All the other studios had abandoned that part of the industry, for television had changed moviegoing habits irrevocably. There was no demand for two-reel films to precede features, and comedians moved to television. In fact, the Stooges comedies had been subtly changing their shooting schedules, which came to resemble those of television situation comedies. Most were shot in one to four days, and the finished product was about 15 minutes long, about 2 to 5 minutes shorter than previous shorts. The budgets were cut as well, and the directors increasingly made use of old footage intercut with new scenes. In some of the old footage, keen observers have spotted a portrait of Shemp on the wall or identified his voice coming from offstage.

On December 20, 1957, the Stooges finished their 197th short for Columbia. It proved to be their last. Cohn decided to close the short-film division for good, marking the end of an era. Nevertheless, Cohn would never dream of wasting money. Columbia had released 8 of the 16 films with Moe, Larry, and Joe in 1957, and would release 6 in 1958 and 2 more in 1959.

Moe, Larry, and Joe's contract had ended. For Moe and Larry, it was the first time in 24 years their contract had not been renewed. Their association with Columbia was the longest such arrangement in show business history. Besser had spent 14 years at Columbia. All were saddened, but Joe was a bit relieved. In November 1957, Besser's beloved wife, Ernie, had had a heart attack, and he was glad to be able to take time off to help her recover at home. The title of his autobiography (_Not Just a Stooge_) notwithstanding, he later

On December 8, 1984, Joe Besser holds his autobiography, _Not Just a Stooge_, and points to himself while posing with an enlarged photograph of the Three Stooges taken when he was a member of the act. In his book, Besser recalled his 64 years as a star in vaudeville, on Broadway, in movies, on radio, and on television.

referred to his time spent as a Stooge as "the happiest years of my life in show business." Moe, ever the businessman, was so financially secure that he did not need to work. Larry, ever the genial, lighthearted partygoer and host, faced poverty and even bankruptcy.

The Three Stooges could have come to an end then. When Moe suggested a personal appearance tour, mostly to help Larry get on his feet financially, Besser declined, citing his wife's health. (When she recovered, he went on to continue a successful career in television and as a voice-over artist in Saturday morning cartoons.) Larry may have needed the money, but perhaps Moe needed the work. His energy was unflagging, and comedy was his lifeblood. He started the search for another Stooge and another way to bring the Stooges' inimitable brand of humor to life again.

7 Oil's Well That Ends Well

THE NEXT STOOGE was a rotund comedian named Joe DeRita, whom Moe and Larry approached in 1958 when he was working for the Minsky theater operation in Las Vegas, Nevada. Joe was born Joe Wardell in Philadelphia, Pennsylvania, on July 12, 1909. His background was different from the Stooges' and Joe Besser's; he had come from a show business family and had been performing onstage with his mother and his sister in the DeRita Sisters and Junior act before he was 10 years old. The bulk of his work in the 1920s and 1930s was in burlesque, or live variety shows. Despite the contemporary connotations of the word, *burlesque* was considered more family-oriented than vaudeville at that time. He recalled that by 1921, "My type of vaudeville was gone. I never worked too risqué."

In the 1940s he worked in feature films for Warner Bros., MGM, and Paramount and performed with Bing Crosby, among others, in United Servicemen's Organization (USO) shows entertaining soldiers during World War II. He was also well known to members of the Columbia team, having

In June 1963, Curly-Joe DeRita, Moe Howard, and Larry Fine appear in a promotional tour for their movie *The Three Stooges Go Around the World in a Daze*. DeRita joined the group in 1958, just after Columbia released Stooges shorts to television.

starred in four short films for that studio between 1946 and 1948. The first, *Slappily Married* (1946), was directed by Ed Bernds, partly written by Elwood Ullman, and featured Christine McIntyre and Symona Boniface among the supporting actors. The film was followed by the Joe DeRita series of three shorts. Two were directed by Jules White and one by Ed Bernds; the writers included Elwood Ullman and Felix Adler; and Sitka, Boniface, and McIntyre appeared in them as well.

By choosing Joe DeRita, the Stooges reached out once again to a member of the familiar Columbia group who had worked with each other throughout the years. The studio was not merely a machine, however, and did not churn out cookie-cutter work. Each actor had different strengths that were used to very specific advantage. In the *Three Stooges Journal,* Michael Eder observed that Joe DeRita developed a funny, suffering, "Milquetoast-type character. Joe's humor was always less broad than that of the other five Stooges; and so his shorts, though physical, have a milder flavor to them." In Bruskin's 1983 interview with Jules White, White opined: "I have nothing against DeRita as a person; he was a nice enough fellow, but he didn't have the same characteristics that Besser had. Besser was dainty and DeRita was a little more the butcher with the cleaver."

Moe and Joe recall varying accounts of the first appearance of the reconstituted Three Stooges. In an interview with Joe Wallison, DeRita stated that his first appearance with them was at a Marine base near San Diego; Moe wrote in his memoirs that it was at a Holiday Inn in Bakersfield, California. Both recall the Bakersfield appearance, in October 1958, as disastrous. The patrons responded so negatively that the club owner wanted to reduce the Stooges' pay. Norman Maurer, Moe's son-in-law, convinced the owner to keep to the original agreement.

Despite the disappointment in Bakersfield, the Stooges were on the brink of a breakthrough. Columbia owned a huge library of old films and shorts and formed a television subsidiary, Screen Gems, to lease these properties to television. In January 1958, Screen Gems put together a package of 78 old Three Stooges comedies for television release. The shorts were marketed as children's television, much as MGM and Warner Bros. cartoons were. Few of these live-action or animated shorts had been specifically created for children; rather, they were made for theater audiences of all ages. Silly faces and goofy stunts could entertain the children, and the quick wordplay and puns from old vaudeville routines kept the adults laughing.

Children immediately fell in love with the antics of the trio. Throughout 1958, the Stooges' popularity quickly grew. Wherever the comedies were aired, they soon became the number-one-rated children's show. The rerelease also led to a new look for Joe, whose size and grace made him resemble Curly but whose hair was styled much like Shemp's. In the late 1980s he told Joe Wallison, "The kids would look at me funny and wonder who is this guy. I was fat like Curly, but had hair like Shemp. . . . I felt the kids could not relate to which Stooge I was and I suggested shaving my head and calling myself Curly-Joe."

The Stooges' next big personal appearance after Bakersfield, featuring Curly-Joe's new persona, was scheduled for the Holiday House in Pittsburgh, Pennsylvania. Stooges shorts were airing on station WTAE there, and the Stooges' visit was a resounding success. Originally booked for one week, they were held over for three more, doing standing-room-only shows filled with children and parents. Agents competed to book their in-person appearances, and the Stooges' salaries skyrocketed. Columbia released a collection of Stooges shorts with Besser as

In the 1959 feature film *Have Rocket, Will Travel,* Curly-Joe, Moe, and Larry perform their antics in space suits. Although the critics panned the movie, children loved watching the trio's pranks, and the Three Stooges' career was reborn.

a feature called *The Three Stooges Fun-O-Rama* in 1959, while Screen Gems released 40 more shorts to television.

Despite the profits—nearly $12 million—that rolled into Columbia following the two initial Stooges' television releases, not one of the Stooges received a penny. Because of the ruling of the president of the Screen Actors' Guild, former B-movie star Ronald Reagan (and later 40th president of the United States), no actor appearing in a film released before 1960 could receive any money from television showings. Moe, Larry, Curly's heirs, Shemp's heirs, and Joe Besser were not entitled to any residuals (money paid to performers for repeated showings of their work). All the money filled the coffers at Columbia.

Still, the Stooges were not reluctant to join forces with the studio again. Columbia offered them a chance to star in a feature for the first time in eight years, and the Stooges accepted. *Have Rocket, Will Travel,* released in 1959, was well received by the moviegoing public but did not gain critical raves. Although the Stooges' antics held up well over 15 minutes or so of a two-reeler, the story and skits seemed to wind down over the course of an hour and a half. But the children, who made up the majority of the Stooges' feature-film audience, loved them. Dismayed by Columbia's decision to cobble together a series of Curly shorts with linking footage by noted ventriloquist Paul Winchell (released as *Stop! Look! Laugh!* in 1960), the trio decided to work with Twentieth Century-Fox–and sued Columbia. Eventually, Norman Maurer took over the Stooges' management, and an out-of-court settlement was reached.

The feature for Fox, *Snow White and the Three Stooges,* went disastrously over budget. The 1961 film is described by Leslie Halliwell in *Halliwell's Film and Video Guide* as "surprisingly tolerable as a holiday attraction, once you get over the shock." The next feature, produced by Norman Maurer and directed by Ed Bernds, was *The Three Stooges Meet Hercules,* for Columbia. Released in 1962, it was a humorous take on the series of popular Italian-made Hercules films of the time. (Currently, the Hercules films have attained a new popularity on cable television as hilarious camp oddities.)

Larry, Curly-Joe, and Moe, with clothespins on their noses, react to a skunk. Displeased with Columbia's release of a film in 1960 made up of a series of shorts with Curly, the Three Stooges sued Columbia and signed with Twentieth Century–Fox.

The Three Stooges Go Around the World in a Daze (1963) was among several feature-length films the trio agreed to do for Columbia Pictures, with whom the Stooges had reconciled. In spite of the success and popularity of their films during the 1960s, the Three Stooges did not receive raves from critics for their work.

The Stooges feature was exceedingly popular and was followed by three more full-length films for Columbia, in 1962, 1963, and 1965. Always the family man, Moe allowed his grandson Jeffrey Maurer backstage to witness what went on behind the scenes, something that was not common practice in the industry.

Despite the success of the films, Curly-Joe DeRita and Joe Besser never received the critical credit that Curly and Shemp had. The general consensus seemed to be that the quality of the Stooges' work had been disintegrating steadily since the deaths of Curly and Shemp. Television writer Stephen Cox, author of *The Hooterville Handbook*

In November 1973, actors George Montgomery (left) and Aldo Ray flank Larry Fine, who is in a wheelchair, while attending a movie premiere in Hollywood. Fine enthusiastically entertained everyone he met, including his fellow patients at the Motion Picture Country Home and Hospital, until his death in 1975.

and *The Official Abbott & Costello Scrapbook,* wrote in the Fall 1993 *Three Stooges Journal,* "[Curly-]Joe's sense of humor was never realized in any Stooge vehicle, although he had a genuine quick wit, straight out of the old show biz era. His timing was good, and he could get a bit raunchy at times, but like Joe Besser, he was funnier solo."

Throughout the late 1950s and early 1960s, Three Stooges–related merchandise became extremely popular. Comic books, games, hats, balloons, and the first Three Stooges Fan Club brought in thousands of dollars. An able manager and a comic book artist in his own right, Norman Maurer developed many of the ideas and strategies for the comics and carefully licensed the Stooges' likenesses. The trio's fortunes had turned for the better.

They appeared in a cameo as firemen in *It's a Mad, Mad, Mad, Mad World,* a star-studded romp released in 1963 featuring such old-time Stooges cohorts as Jimmy Durante, Milton Berle, Zasu Pitts, and Phil Silvers as well

In October 1972, Moe Howard poses with his wife, Helen. While battling lung cancer, Howard wrote his amusing autobiography, *Moe Howard and the 3 Stooges,* which was published in 1977, two years after his death.

as Ethel Merman, Peter Falk, and Buster Keaton. Additionally, the Stooges appeared in *Four for Texas,* an undistinguished 1963 Western comedy starring Frank Sinatra and Dean Martin. Movie reviewer Judith Crist claimed "the major laughs come from the Three Stooges doing an ancient routine."

An animated series called "The New Three Stooges" was syndicated in October 1965. Consisting of 156 short cartoons and 40 new live-action sequences combined into 39 half-hour shows, the series featured Ed Bernds as the director and screenwriter in the live-action sequences, with Norman Maurer as producer. In this new live material, Emil Sitka returned as the Stooges' favorite sidekick.

In the late 1960s, commercial interest in the Three Stooges waned. Personal tragedy struck Larry. His beloved wife, Mabel, died on May 30, 1967, while the Stooges were touring. Still, the Stooges continued on. In 1970, Norman Maurer helped the trio with what was to be their last attempt at a feature film. He wrote the story and screenplay and also served as producer and director. The film, *Kook's Tour,* was never completed. (Videotapes of an edited, shortened version of the unfinished film exist but are extremely rare.) During the shooting, on January 9, 1970, Larry had a paralyzing stroke. His film career over, he retired to the Motion Picture Country Home and Hospital, where he spent the next five years entertaining fellow patients and occasionally appearing at neighboring California colleges to lecture. On January 24, 1975, Larry Fine died.

During the early 1970s, Moe visited Larry regularly and appeared on the popular television talk show "The Mike Douglas Show" several times, even engaging in gently humorous pie-throwing escapades with his wife, Helen. Moe's health worsened gradually, though he remained active. On May 4, 1975, he succumbed to lung cancer and died. Although he knew he was sick, he never discussed his illness publicly. Through the last years of his life he kept up a schedule of popular campus appearances and found time to produce a wonderfully entertaining memoir, *Moe Howard and the 3 Stooges,* which was published posthumously in 1977. After 50 years of entertaining America, the Three Stooges were no more—but their legacy was far from over.

8 All the World's a Stooge

IT IS NEARLY IMPOSSIBLE for the average American citizen to go a week without somehow coming into contact with some aspect of the Three Stooges. While changing the channels one can find reruns of the Stooges' shorts on a number of local stations or cable superstations, being shown at any time of day. The children's favorite "Three Blind Mice" has come to be associated with the Stooges, and the opening notes are almost sure to presage a clip from one of the shorts. Popular syndicated comic strips such as "Momma," "Wizard of Id," and "The Far Side" have featured jokes about the Three Stooges. For example, in the February 21, 1994, "Far Side" daily calendar entry, cartoonist Gary Larson sketched Mount Rushmore featuring Moe giving Curly an eye poke alongside Larry and captioned it "At Mount Stoogemore." Clips of Moe, Larry, and Curly pop up in national television commercials for health care companies and other products. And a 1994 television commercial for iced tea features actor David Carradine (of "Kung

---

Larry, Curly-Joe, and Moe arrive at the Paramount Theatre in New York for a gala charity premiere in May 1960. Televising Three Stooges shorts and movies on local and cable stations in the 1990s has made the trio very popular to audiences once again.

93

Fu" fame) fighting for his drink using face slaps and eye pokes as a new kind of martial art. Jay Leno, Garry Shandling, David Letterman, and countless other stand-up comedians regularly make Stooges references in their material. Leno has often claimed that if you ask women to name their heros, they will name women who have improved the world, whereas men will invariably name an athlete, an actor, and a Stooge. Walking down the street one can look into a shop window and see Stooges statues, ties, action figures, dolls, posters, or T-shirts. And Curly homages can also be found in major Hollywood films, being performed by such stars as Mel Gibson in the *Lethal Weapon* movies and John Candy, as "the lean, mean fighting machine" Dewey Oxenberger in the 1981 film *Stripes.*

Turn on the radio and the Stooges' influence continues. The rock group the Del-Lords named themselves after the Stooges' longtime director. Bruce Springsteen, when nearing the end of his legendary four-hour concerts, often falls to the floor, clutching his guitar, and rolls around in a circle in a mock-Curly dance. Even Bob Dylan, who usually sprinkles his songs with references to poets and philosophers, both famous and obscure, mentions Moe. In the 1965 song "Highway 61," Dylan sings of how the fleeing Georgia Sam asks Moe Howard which way to go, and Howard replies by pointing his gun, sending him down Highway 61. On his 1993 album *Bat out of Hell II: Back into Hell,* Meat Loaf sings, in the song "Everything Louder Than Everything Else," that the three men he admires most are Curly, Larry, and Moe. And even Jack Kerouac, the Beat generation author of *On the Road,* recorded "Visions of Neal: Neal and the Three Stooges" (a slightly different version appears in the book *Visions of Cody*), in which Kerouac tells in his bebop style about imitating the "stagger of the Stooges," talks about the "nose yanks, blap, bloop, going, going, gong" of their

gags, and imagines the Stooges "providing scenes for wild vibrating hysterias as great as the hysterias of hipsters at Jazz at the Philharmonics."

The Three Stooges even touched the life of pop superstar Michael Jackson. Jackson contributed the foreword

Curly Howard, dressed in drag for one of the Three Stooges shorts, is considered to be the funniest Stooge by most fans today.

95

to Joan Howard Maurer's 1985 book about her uncle, *Curly: An Illustrated Biography of the Superstooge.* In it Jackson wrote, "In my childhood, around our home in Indiana, it was a daily ritual for me to watch the Three Stooges on television. All my brothers loved them then and even more so now." Jackson has a particular fondness for Curly, whom he thought "had a magic. He was God-gifted—a natural. Even when he didn't intend to be funny he was magic." About the group in general Jackson wrote, "The Stooges' craziness helped me to relax and to

Curly has his hands squeezed in a vise by Moe and Larry. The Stooges' portrayal of physical violence, such as beatings with hammers, scorching with irons, eye pokes, etc., has worried many people who are concerned about its ill effect on children.

escape life's burdens. They influenced me so much that I even wrote a song about them."

The Stooges' antics still can be heard echoing in the hallowed halls of Congress as the debate about violence on television grows. As television networks, congressional leaders, local stations, and the Parent-Teacher Association (PTA) groups argue about what constitutes violence on television, the Three Stooges are mentioned frequently. Although the violence in Stooges films had come under scrutiny since the first release of the Colum-

bia shorts on television in 1958, the debate became even louder in the 1980s as the nation grew more conscious of the violence both in society and on television. On March 4, 1983, the *New York Times,* in an article entitled "Three Stooges Nostalgia Is Today's Newest Fad," discussed the issue of violence in Stooges films. A whole new young audience was being introduced to the Stooges as a result of the resurgent popularity of the shorts shown on television; popularity that was, to some extent, a result of the enthusiasm of young television executives and baby boomers who had grown up on the Stooges in the late 1950s and early 1960s. According to the writer of the *New York Times* article,

Fred Ferretti, the shorts "have not only kept [the Stooges] very much alive but have become the core of one of the latest fads in our fad-ridden country." In the *New York Times* story, Ira Friedman, who helped organize the Official Three Stooges Fan Club, said, "Everybody wants a piece of them, a piece of nostalgia. And more and more you see other comics aping them. Critics say they were violent, but by today's standards they're mild. Their violence was immediate and not lasting, not brutal. It was slapstick, good clean fun." Two years later, in May 1985, the *Wall Street Journal* reported that WPIX-TV in New York was editing the Stooges' films, cutting out the eye pokes, which were "deemed too harsh under the station's anti-mayhem policy."

The current raging debate about the depiction of violence on television, spearheaded by Illinois senator Paul Simon and people such as the Reverend Donald Wildmon (whose American Family organization attempts to monitor television by imposing its own moral values on what is watched), centers on nudity, drug use, guns, rape, and murder. Yet somehow the Stooges, with their face slaps, eye pokes, and other slapstick gags, seem to get dragged into the argument against violence. The inclusion of the Stooges in the war against violence on television led *TV Guide,* in its January 29, 1994, "Cheers 'n' Jeers" column, to decry "Chicago's WPWR-TV, for deciding that before airing 'Three Stooges' shorts, violence disclaimers were needed. . . . [O]ur measured response—given our interest in solving some of the very real problems of TV violence—is: *nyuk, nyuk, nyuk.* "

What Fred Ferretti referred to in 1983 as a "fad" is still raging. That year did see a resurgence in the Stooges' popularity. After a long battle to get the Three Stooges a star on the Hollywood Walk of Fame, they finally received their due. The Walk of Fame, stretching across both sides of Hollywood Boulevard and Vine Street in Hollywood, California, offers the opportunity for stars of radio, film, and television to have a star with their name on it placed on the popular streets. (First the chamber of commerce must approve a star, and then the entertainer, or his or her estate, must agree to pay, to date, a $3,500 fee to actually receive it.) It is an honor generally reserved for what many perceive as the upper echelon of American entertainment. (Although foreigners do receive stars, it is interesting to note that even such a glamorous, beloved international star as Sophia Loren, who had been acting for more than 40 years, had to wait until February 1, 1994, to receive her place on the Walk of Fame, next to Paul Newman). Among the famous names lining the streets of Hollywood, passing in front of such famous places as Mann's Chinese Theatre and the Hollywood Roosevelt Hotel, are Marilyn Monroe, Jackie Gleason, George Burns, Milton Berle, Jimmy Durante, and Clark Gable, although in recent years less-famous and less-enduring entertainers have been added. Yet for many years the Stooges were ignored, despite the support of tens of thousands of letters and even an organization, A Star for the Three Stooges Committee. It was believed that the Stooges' humor was thought to be too lowbrow to add the group to the prestigious   Walk of Fame.

But finally, on August 30, 1983, near 1560 Vine Street, the Three Stooges finally received their star, after 1,766 other stars had already been given out. Moe, Larry, Curly, and Shemp, unfortunately, were no longer alive to witness this event, and Curly-Joe could not attend because of ill health. Moe had been so annoyed that the Stooges had not received their star that in 1975 he had said, "They can keep their star, and I'll tell them where to put it—one point at a time." Of the six Stooges, only Joe Besser was able to attend. But he was among thou-

sands of friends. More people appeared to see this star unveiled than had shown up at any previous unveiling. Milton Berle was on hand to give a speech, and he said, "What these men gave to the world is timeless. These great gentlemen, who brought laughter to millions and millions of people, will never be forgotten."

There seems to be no stopping the popularity of the Stooges. Throughout the 1980s and 1990s, their fan base keeps expanding as they gain more and more critical success. In the 1980s there were two successful national Three Stooges fan clubs, and one of them, The Three Stooges Fan Club, Inc., is still flourishing today. Three Stooges film festivals are shown throughout the United States, often to standing-room-only business. Yearly conventions are held in Pennsylvania, where thousands of Stooges knuckleheads buy and sell rare Stooges merchandise, exchange their favorite Stooges stories, and attend screenings of rare Stooges films. (They also have raging debates about who the best Stooge was, with the vast majority supporting Curly.) The 1985 film *Stoogemania* featured Josh Mostel in an asylum reserved for people with Stooges-related illnesses—people who thought they were Shemp or who could not stop saying "nyuk-nyuk-nyuk." The MGM Grand Hotel and Casino in Las Vegas, Nevada, has established a live stage act in honor of the Stooges. There was even a Three Stooges Deli in Hammond, Louisiana, that featured not only Stooges memorabilia but dishes such as Curly's Combo and the Stooges Sub.

In 1984, the Stooges' surprise renaissance reached new heights as a song by a little-known group called Jump 'n the Saddle broke into the top 20 on the music charts, and the accompanying video became an MTV favorite, featuring a montage of Curly's most hilarious antics. The song, "The Curly Shuffle," has since sold more than 1 million copies and helped propel Stoogemania.

OPPOSITE:
Joe Besser (center) waves to the heavens after the unveiling of the Three Stooges star on the Hollywood Walk of Fame on August 30, 1983. Joining him at the ceremony are Joan Howard Maurer (squatting, far left), daughter of Moe Howard, and Jean DeRita (kneeling next to Besser), wife of Curly-Joe, who was ill and could not attend.

In the midst of this revival of interest in the Stooges, Joe Besser died, on March 1, 1988, after a six-month illness. He was 80 years old. Although the Stooges films he had appeared in were not the group's most famous, he was alive to cherish the growing popularity of the group as a whole. He loved getting fan mail and making personal appearances. Despite his initial resentment about being known as a Stooge when he had done so much more in his career, Besser finally learned to appreciate the connection. In fact, when his autobiography was originally published in 1985, it was called *Not Just a Stooge;* however, when it was released in a smaller paperback version in 1990, after his death, it was entitled *Once a Stooge, Always a Stooge.* The new edition even featured a revised ending in which Besser wrote, "I am deeply thankful for my association with the Three Stooges. In every sense, my years with them turned out to be a blessing. I'll be the first to admit that, for years, it bothered me that my Stooge role overshadowed some other great work in my career. But as time has passed and I've mellowed with age, I realize that thanks to the Stooges and my association with them, fans are able to appreciate my work with the boys and rediscover my other work."

Yet another accolade was added to the Stooges' canon when they received the Lifetime Achievement Award at the 1993 MTV Movie Awards. Not to be confused with an Oscar, the award was presented by actor Mel Gibson, who followed his short speech honoring the boys by hitting himself over the head with an enormous wrench.

The last Stooge, Curly-Joe DeRita, passed away on July 3, 1993. Like Joe Besser, he had enjoyed being remembered as a Stooge in his later years, and he received thousands of letters from fans and lots of visitors who wanted to talk about his time as a Stooge. Some people argue that the Three Stooges died after Moe Howard died; others say that they died after Joe Besser died. But writer Stephen Cox wrote, in the Fall 1994 *Three Stooges Journal*, "It really hit me when Joe [DeRita] died, because not only did a kindly man leave, but it was the finalization of the Stooges on earth. The last Stooge died."

By means of film festivals, conventions, television, books, homages, and memorabilia, the Three Stooges will probably be remembered forever. They amused America at a time when Americans were hungry for diversion, and they continue to entertain generations of people around the world decades later. Their films have been dubbed into numerous foreign languages, and their mark can be seen in films and television to this day. How they are remembered, however, is perhaps the final Stooges debate. Throughout their career critics considered them second-level performers, below the ranks of Laurel and Hardy, the Marx Brothers, Charlie Chaplin, and Abbott and Costello. Yet their films, their gags, and their faces are arguably more well known today than any of the other famous comedians of their time. James Rahn wrote in the July 1990 issue of *Philadelphia* magazine that "the Stooges don't get much critical acclaim . . . even though their comedy series has lasted longer than any other, because they're perceived as too violent— paradoxically, the same reason they have so many fans. . . . They recognized the universal appeal of aggression. They took the frenetic and wildly rowdy nature of America and turned it into a lampoon. That was their genius."

But it was not just their supposed physical rambunctiousness that affected their critical popularity. Film critics generally do not include the Stooges with the greats of film comedy. But their millions of fans do. One such fan, actor-comedian Martin Short, told the *Calgary Herald* that the Three Stooges "are undervalued. You see some of the physical stunts that these guys do, and it's incredibly funny. . . . People don't give it the respect it deserves. . . . Sure there's a critical contempt for [t]he

Three Stooges, and it's a pity that people don't value this kind of comedy."

In the end, of course, it does not matter what the critics say, what various organizations claim is violent or objectionable, or what the many books argue about the cinematic and historic value of the Three Stooges. All that really matters is what six very funny men left the world: hundreds of hours of eye pokes, pie fights, "nyuk-nyuk-nyuks," and "heep-heep-heeps" that have made millions of people the world over break out into enduring fits of hysterical laughter.

Further Reading ★ ★ ★ ★ ★ ★ ★ ★ ★ ★ ★ ★ ★ ★

Behind the Three Stooges: The White Brothers. Conversations with David N. Bruskin. Edited by David N. Bruskin. Los Angeles: Directors Guild of America, 1993.

Besser, Joseph, with Greg Lenburg and Jeff Lenburg. *Not Just a Stooge.* Orange, CA: Excelsior, 1984. Revised edition. *Once a Stooge, Always a Stooge.* New York: Knightsbridge, 1990.

Feinberg, Morris. *Larry: The Stooge in the Middle.* San Francisco: Last Gasp of San Francisco, 1984.

Halliwell, Leslie. *Halliwell's Film and Video Guide.* New York: Scribner's, 1986.

Hansen, Tom, with Jeffrey Forrester. *Stoogemania.* Chicago: Contemporary Books, 1984.

Howard, Moe. *Moe Howard and the 3 Stooges.* Secaucus, NJ: Stuart, 1977.

Katz, Ephraim. *The Film Encyclopedia.* New York: Crowell, 1979.

Lassin, Gary, ed. *The Three Stooges Journal.* Gwynedd Valley, PA: Three Stooges Fan Club.

Lenburg, Jeff, with Joan Howard Maurer and Greg Lenburg. *The Three Stooges Scrapbook.* New York: Carol, 1982.

Maurer, Joan Howard. *Curly: An Illustrated Biography of the Superstooge.* New York: Carol, 1985.

VIDEOS

The Lost Stooges. Turner Home Entertainment, 1990.

Love Those Stooges. Superior Promotions, 1993.

The Stooges: Lost and Found! Madhouse Video, 1987.

The Three Stooges compilation videos. Columbia Pictures.

Filmography ★★★★★★★★★★★★★★★★★★★★

The Three Stooges made more than 200 films together. The following is a selective list of some of their craziest and most important films, many of which are available on various video compilations.

MOE, LARRY, AND CURLY WITH
    TED HEALY

Soup to Nuts, Fox, 1930. Stooges' first film.

Nertsery Rhymes, MGM, 1933. Stooges' first film for MGM, shot in experimental color.

Beer and Pretzels, MGM, 1933. The Stooges play comedians thrown out of a theater.

MOE, LARRY, AND CURLY

Woman Haters, Columbia, 1934. Stooges' first film for Columbia.

Punch Drunks, Columbia, 1934. Boxing film heavily scripted by Moe.

Men in Black, Columbia, 1934. The Stooges play bumbling interns—the only Stooges film to be nominated for an Academy Award.

Hoi Polloi, Columbia, 1935. The Stooges are part of a bet to see whether environment or heredity determines an individual's social class.

You Nazty Spy, Columbia, 1940. Moe's favorite, in which the Stooges satirize Hitler and the Nazis in the land of Moronica.

A-Plumbing We Will Go, Columbia, 1940. Outstanding comedy that features a hysterical Curly bit as a plumber trying to fix some pipes while a fancy party is going on.

All the World's a Stooge, Columbia, 1941. The Stooges are "adopted" by a wealthy couple.

Half-Wit's Holiday, Columbia, 1947. Curly's last film as a Stooge and Emil Sitka's first.

MOE, LARRY, AND SHEMP

Fright Night, Columbia, 1947. Shemp's first and favorite film.

Hold That Lion, Columbia, 1947. Curly appears in a cameo role.

Brideless Groom, Columbia, 1947. Shemp must get married to inherit a fortune and has sidesplitting run-ins with old girlfriends.

Punchy Cowpunchers, Columbia, 1950. The Stooges in the Old West.

Corny Casanovas, Columbia, 1952. One by one, all three Stooges propose to the same woman—as each one hides in a different part of the woman's apartment.

Spooks and *Pardon My Backfire,* Columbia, 1953. The only 3-D Stooges films.

For Crimin' Out Loud, Columbia, 1956. Shemp's final film (followed by four films featuring old footage and body doubles).

★ ★

MOE, LARRY, AND JOE

Hoofs and Goofs, Columbia, 1957. Joe Besser's first film as a Stooge, featuring Tony the Wonder Horse.

A Merry Mix-Up, Columbia, 1957. The Stooges play three sets of identical triplets separated at birth who suddenly all find each other.

The Three Stooges Fun-O-Rama, Columbia, 1959. Feature film made up of shorts; widely promoted at the time.

MOE, LARRY, AND CURLY-JOE

Have Rocket, Will Travel, Columbia, 1959. Joe DeRita's first film as a Stooge and the Stooges' first full-length film in eight years.

The Outlaws Is Coming!, Columbia, 1965. The Stooges' last full-length film, featuring many familiar television personalities as famous gunfighters.

Chronology ★ ★ ★ ★ ★ ★ ★ ★ ★ ★ ★ ★ ★ ★ ★ ★ ★

March 17, 1895	Shemp Howard is born Samuel Horwitz in Brooklyn, New York
June 19, 1897	Moe Howard is born Moses Horwitz in Brooklyn, New York
October 5, 1902	Larry Fine is born Louis Feinberg in Philadelphia, Pennsylvania
October 22, 1903	Curly Howard is born Jerome Lester Horwitz in Brooklyn, New York
August 12, 1907	Joseph Besser is born in St. Louis, Missouri
July 12, 1909	Joe DeRita is born Joseph Wardell in Philadelphia
1909	Moe makes his screen debut as Harry Moses Horwitz in *We Must Do Our Best*
1914	Moe joins Captain Billy Bryant's stock company
1922	Moe and Shemp join comedian Ted Healy's act at Brooklyn's Prospect Theater in New York
1925	Larry joins Healy, Moe, and Shemp on the vaudeville circuit
1929	In May, Healy, Moe, Larry, and Shemp appear in the Broadway revue *A Night in Venice*
1930	*Soup to Nuts,* a Twentieth Century–Fox film featuring Healy, Moe, Larry, and Shemp, is released. After the film, the trio leaves Healy
1932	The three rejoin Healy for J. J. Shubert's *The Passing Show of 1932;* Shemp leaves the act for a solo film career and is replaced by Curly
1933–34	Healy and His Stooges appear in Metro-Goldwyn-Mayer shorts and full-length features
1934	Moe, Larry, and Curly break with Healy and sign a contract with Columbia Pictures studio to star in shorts as the Three Stooges
1947	After appearing in 97 shorts, Curly suffers a career-ending stroke and is replaced by Shemp

★ ★

1951   The Stooges star in a full-length feature, *Gold Raiders*

1952   Curly dies on January 18

1955   Shemp dies of a heart attack on November 23, having appeared in 78 shorts

1956   On January 1, Joe Besser joins the act as the third Stooge

1957   On November 20, the Stooges' Columbia contract is not renewed; Joe Besser retires from the Stooges' act

1958   Columbia, under its Screen Gems division, releases 78 shorts to television; the Stooges' popularity soars; Joe DeRita joins as the third Stooge

1959–63   The Three Stooges make five feature films and numerous personal appearances

1965   The animated *New Three Stooges* syndicated television series appears

1970   *Kook's Tour,* a feature, is partially completed; during filming, Larry suffers a stroke and retires

1975   Larry dies on January 24

1975   Moe dies on May 4

1983   On August 30, the Three Stooges receive a star on the Hollywood Walk of Fame; in December, the novelty song "The Curly Shuffle" jumps to number one on the Billboard chart, marking a resurgence of interest in the Stooges

1988   Joe Besser dies on March 1

1993   Joe DeRita, the last Stooge, dies on July 3

1993 to present   The Three Stooges shorts continue to be shown on television; the Stooges receive a Lifetime Achievement Award at the MTV Movie Awards, presented by Stooges fanatic Mel Gibson; the group's antics are mimicked by famous actors in major Hollywood films; film clips are used in national advertising campaigns; Stooges' heirs bicker over various payments

Index ★★★★★★★★★★★★★★★★★★★★★★★★

★ ★

Mark and Ellen Scordato have written several books for children and young adults, including works on Sarah Winnemucca and Argentina. Mark, a former member of the Three Stooges Fan Club, has a master's degree in cinema studies from New York University; Ellen is a graduate of Wellesley College. They live in New York City with their cat, Goat.

Leeza Gibbons is a reporter for and cohost of the nationally syndicated television program "Entertainment Tonight" and NBC's daily talk show "Leeza." A graduate of the University of South Carolina's School of Journalism, Gibbons joined the on-air staff of "Entertainment Tonight" in 1984 after cohosting WCBS-TV's "Two on the Town" in New York City. Prior to that, she cohosted "PM Magazine" on WFAA-TV in Dallas, Texas, and on KFDM-TV in Beaumont, Texas. Gibbons also hosts the annual "Miss Universe," "Miss U.S.A.," and "Miss Teen U.S.A." pageants, as well as the annual Hollywood Christmas Parade. She is active in a number of charities and has served as the national chairperson for the Spinal Muscular Atrophy Division of the Muscular Dystrophy Association; each September, Gibbons cohosts the National MDA Telethon with Jerry Lewis.

PICTURE CREDITS

AP/Wide World Photos: pp. 86, 100; Archive Photos: pp. 10, 52–53, 62, 68, 78, 87, 89, 90, 92; The Bettmann Archive: pp. 23, 33, 80; The Brooklyn Historical Society: pp. 20–21, 26; Photofest: pp. 2, 12, 13, 16, 19, 24, 28, 34, 39, 42–43, 46, 49, 50, 60, 64, 67, 71, 74, 88, 95, 96–97; UPI/Bettmann: pp. 44, 59, 82; Marc Wanamaker, Bison Archives: p. 14.